MW00715567

10 Minute Guide to
NetWare®

Galen Grimes

alpha
books

A Division of Prentice Hall Computer Publishing
11711 North College Avenue, Carmel, Indiana 46032 USA

To Joanne, who gives me time to write, and encourages me to do so.

©1993 by Alpha Books

International Standard Book Number: 1-56761-127-3
Library of Congress Catalog Card Number: 92-75158

96   95   94   93   8   7   6   5   4   3   2   1

Interpretation of the printing code: the rightmost number of the first series of numbers is the year of the book's printing; the rightmost number of the second series of numbers is the number of the book's printing. For example, a printing code of 93-1 shows that the first printing of the book occurred in 1993.

Publisher: *Marie Butler-Knight*
Associate Publisher: *Lisa A. Bucki*
Managing Editor: *Elizabeth Keaffaber*
Acquisitions Manager: *Stephen Poland*
Development Editor: *Seta Frantz*
Manuscript Editor: *Barry Childs-Helton*
Cover Designer: *Dan Armstrong*
Designer: *Amy Peppler-Adams*
Indexer: *Jeanne Clark*
Production Team: *Diana Bigham, Scott Cook, Tim Cox, Mark Enochs, Tom Loveman, Joe Ramon, Carrie Roth, Greg Simsic, Barbara Webster*

Screen reproductions in this book were created by means of the program Collage Plus from Inner Media, Inc., Hollis, NH.

Special thanks to James P. McCarter for ensuring the technical accuracy of this book.

Trademarks

Contents

iv

Introduction

The computer in front of you is no longer an island unto itself. It has been connected to something called a Novell NetWare *local area network*, and you are anxious to discover what this network is—and how it will improve the operation of your computer.

Simply stated, a network is just a series of computers connected together by hardware and software. The hardware consists of cabling and a special interface card inside each computer. The software is what is called the *network operating system*, which in this case is a series of programs called Novell NetWare, or just simply NetWare.

Once everything is installed and running, you will find many advantages to using NetWare:

* As a network user, you can share files and programs with other users on the network.

* You can send messages to other users on the network.

* You can use any number of printers, plotters, or other output devices connected to the network.

- You gain added security for "sensitive or confidential" information, since data and files can be protected from unauthorized users.

What Is the 10 Minute Guide?

The *10 Minute Guide* series is designed to help you learn new programs quickly and easily through a series of lessons, each designed to take about 10 minutes or less. Each lesson will teach you the basic skills you need to log in, and to make the best use of both your time and the resources available on your NetWare network.

Best of all, you do not need to spend long hours laboring through the volumes of NetWare manuals trying to figure out what information you need to learn. All the basic information you need to know is covered in this *10 Minute Guide*.

Conventions Used in This Book

To help you as you move through the lessons, the following conventions are used:

On-screen text	On-screen type will appear in a special computer font
What you type	Information you type will appear in a bold, color computer font.
Items you select	Commands, options, and icons you select (or keys you press) will appear in color.

Key combinations   In many cases you must press a two-key combination in order to enter a command (for example "Press Ctrl-C"). In such cases, hold down the first key, press the second key, then release both together.

In addition, the *10 Minute Guide to NetWare 3.11* uses the following icons to help you identify helpful information:

Panic Button   This icon helps to identify potential problem areas, and usually offers a practical solution.

Timesaver Tip   This icon helps to point out tips for saving time on items or commands you might use often.

Plain English   This icon is used to explain new terms further, in (you guessed it) "plain English."

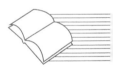

How to Use the 10 Minute Guide

The first three lessons are designed to get you up and running on NetWare quickly. You should take these lessons in the order presented here. After you have finished these lessons, feel free to scan over the other lessons, and take them as you feel they apply to the way your network is set up. Novell NetWare is very flexible; it can be set up to accommodate a variety of needs and usages. Not everything in the *10 Minute Guide to NetWare 3.11* will necessarily apply to your situation.

Lesson 1
Logging In and Out of NetWare

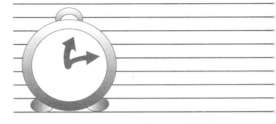

In this lesson you will learn how to log into and log out of a Novell NetWare local area network.

Login or log on?   At times you may see the terms "log in," "login," "log on." They are often used interchangeably. They all refer to the process of informing the file server that you, the network user, will begin using network resources (network drives, network printers, etc.). And as you might have guessed, the terms "log out," "logout," "log off" refer to the process of letting the file server know that you are discontinuing your use of network resources.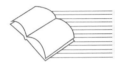

Account IDs and Passwords

Every user on a NetWare network must have an account ID, also known as the *user name*. User names can be up to 47 characters long, and can be characters (A–Z) or numbers (0–9). Passwords are optional. If you are required to enter a password, it is because your network supervisor has included passwords as an additional security precaution. When passwords are used:

1

- They can be up to 128 characters long.

- They can be required to have a minimum length, usually 5 characters.

- Users can be given the option of changing their own passwords.

- The network operating system can be set to force users to change their passwords at a certain interval (such as every 6 months).

- Users can be forced to use a different, unique password every time they change their passwords (if this option is used, the system will remember eight previous passwords, and will not let you reuse them).

Logging Into Your NetWare Network

There are three programs which must be run prior to *logging in*. These should have been installed on your computer by your network supervisor. Often these programs are set to run automatically when you first turn on your computer.

Logging Into NetWare Automatically

1. If your computer is not already on, turn it on.

2. At the `Enter your login name:` prompt, type your account ID and press Enter.

3. At the Enter password: prompt, type your password and press Enter. Your password will not display on the screen. (See Figure 1.1.)

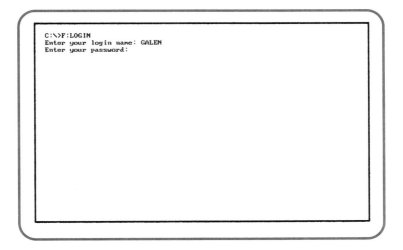

```
C:\>F:LOGIN
Enter your login name: GALEN
Enter your password:
```

Figure 1.1 Logging into NetWare.

Nothing Happened If nothing happened when you turned your computer on, or you don't have an account ID and password? You might have to run the three programs mentioned earlier, manually.

Logging Into NetWare Manually

1. If you need to run the three programs manually, first type IPX and press Enter.

2. Then type NET3 and press Enter. (If you are running DOS version 4.0, type NET4; if you are running DOS 5.0,

3

type NET5. There is also a non-specific DOS version called NETX.) If these two programs run successfully, you are now connected to the file server. (See Figure 1.2.)

```
C>IPX
Novell IPX/SPX v3.82 Rev. A (901218)
(C) Copyright 1985, 1998 Novell Inc.  All Rights Reserved.

LAN Option: 3Com 3c585 EtherLink Plus (Assy 2812)  v4.12EC (910117)
Hardware Configuration: IO: 300; IRQ: 10; DMA: 5 (Jumpers Config)

C>NET3

NetWare V3.22 - Workstation Shell (910731)
(C) Copyright 1991 Novell, Inc.  All Rights Reserved.

Running on DOS V3.31

Attached to server NETWARE_SERVER_1
02-04-93    2:41:45 pm

C>
```

Figure 1.2   Successfully connected to file server.

3. Now type F:LOGIN, and enter your account ID and password.

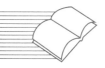

File Servers   The file server is nothing more than another computer where NetWare (the network operating system) is running. As the name implies, the "file servers" are designed to serve (or more precisely, provide services to) the network users, which are referred to as "clients." On a small network, you may have one or two file servers serving 50-100 users/clients. On larger networks, you could conceivably see upwards of a dozen or more file servers serving 500-2000 (or greater users/clients).

4

Your Server Is... The *file server* is nothing more than another computer where NetWare (the network operating system) is running.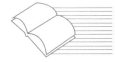

Still Can't Log In If you still failed to log in, contact your network supervisor to get exact instructions on logging in. If you are the network administrator, this book outlines the procedure in an appendix for your convenience (or consult your NetWare instruction manuals).

After you log in, you will be staring at a DOS prompt. If your network supervisor has been busy setting up your network, you could see a *network menu* appear on-screen, listing the programs you can now run, or devices (such as printers) you can now connect to and use. (See Figure 1.3.)

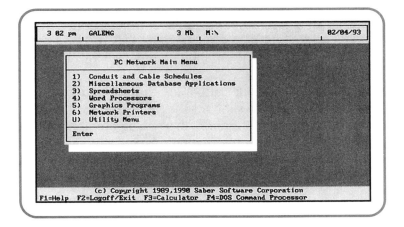

Figure 1.3 Typical network menu.

If you get a menu, spend a few minutes exploring it to see what your network supervisor has set up for you to use. If there is anything you should not use, your network supervisor has probably taken precautions to prevent you from causing any damage.

If no menu appears, you can still spend a few minutes exploring your connection to the file server. Type DIR/P to see what other files or directories are on the network drive you just connected to.

Logging Out

Once again you can use only your individual computer's resources, since you have now "disconnected from" (or logged off from) the network and the network resources.

After you have spent a few minutes exploring the network menu (if there is one), look for a menu option to *log out*. This will disconnect you from the network; once again you can use only your individual computer's resources.

If there is no logout option, look for an option to exit from the menu. This should take you back to the DOS prompt, if you are not already there. You are at the DOS prompt if there is no network menu; type LOGOUT and press Enter. (See Figure 1.4.)

Logout Caution *Do not log out by turning off your computer or rebooting* (pressing Ctrl-Alt-Del). This can cause problems with files or programs you may be using. Likewise, do not simply walk away from your computer without logging out. This defeats the purpose of security (which is why you were given an account ID and password).

```
C:\>logout
GALEN_GRIMES  logged out from server NETWARE_SERVER_1 connection 57.
Login time:    Thursday  February  4, 1993  3:06 pm
Logout time:   Thursday  February  4, 1993  3:06 pm

F:\LOGIN>
```

Figure 1.4   Logging out of the network.

In this lesson, you have learned how to log into your NetWare network and how to log out. In the next lesson, you will learn how to enter a few simple network commands to see how your network is set up.

Lesson 2
NetWare Basics

In this lesson, you will learn to enter a few basic NetWare commands to see how your network is setup. You will see what "drives" are available to you on the file server, and how many file servers you can log into.

Locating Network Drives

On a typical PC you will have two, maybe three disk drives at your disposal. Drive A: is your first floppy disk drive; if you have a second one, it is designated drive B:. Your hard disk is drive C:. One advantage of a network is having the use of more ("network") drives.

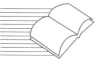

We've Got the Drive   A *network drive* is nothing more than a portion of the hard disk on the file server that has been set up to store files and programs for you and other network users.

If you are not currently logged in, log in the way you did in Lesson 1.

Locating File Servers and Network Drives

Because a file server is simply another computer running NetWare there can be more than one. Logging in takes you to the closest one. To find out if there are other file servers on your network, type SLIST and press Enter. Figure 2.1 shows the information SLIST displays about the file servers it finds.

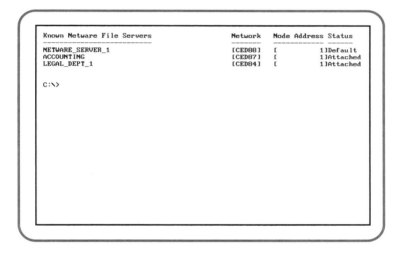

Figure 2.1 SLIST display of file servers.

SLIST displays two types of useful information for you:

- **Known NetWare file servers**   These are the names of the file servers you can log into, provided you have a user ID on the other file servers.

- **Status**   Shows which file servers you are connected to.

Don't worry now about the other file servers. You should be connected to only one, and what you are about to learn will apply not only to it, but to the others as well.

The next step is to find out what drives are available on the server you are logged into. To see the drives, type MAP and press Enter. You should get a display similar to Figure 2.2.

```
F:\>map

Drive  A:    maps to a local disk.
Drive  B:    maps to a local disk.
Drive  C:    maps to a local disk.
Drive  D:    maps to a local disk.
Drive  E:    maps to a local disk.
Drive  F: = NETWARE_SERVER_1\SYS:   \
-------
SEARCH1:    = C:\
SEARCH2:    = C:\DRDOS
SEARCH3:    = C:\NETWARE
SEARCH4:    = Z:. [NETWARE_SERVER_1\SYS:   \UTILITY]
SEARCH5:    = Y:. [NETWARE_SERVER_1\SYS:   \PUBLIC]

F:\>
```

Figure 2.2   MAP command, showing available network drives.

Figure 2.2 shows the default mapping set up by the network supervisor. In later lessons, you will see that the supervisor can give you greater access to network resources as you need them. This is part of network security.

Authorized Personnel Only *Network security* is nothing more than the control the supervisor maintains over network resources (drives, files, printers, etc.) and who is permitted to use these resources.

In Figure 2.2, drives A: through E: are mapped as *local drives* because of the DOS LASTDRIVE=E command (usually in the root directory of your drive C:, in the CONFIG.SYS file). Even if it is not in your CONFIG.SYS file, DOS sets it as the default unless you specify another drive letter for LASTDRIVE=. NetWare begins mapping its network drives on the first drive following the LASTDRIVE= command. In most cases, your first network drive (your *default drive*) is MAPped as F:, as shown in this line:

```
Drive F: = NETWARE_SERVER_1\SYS: \
```

This line also shows the name of the server you logged into (NETWARE_SERVER_1) and the volume you are using.

Two more lines extend your DOS PATH command to include subdirectories on network drive F:. These lines begin with the SEARCH command:

```
SEARCH1:   = Z:. [NETWARE_SERVER_1\SYS: \UTILITY]
SEARCH2:   = Y:. [NETWARE_SERVER_1\SYS: \PUBLIC]
```

Here the subdirectories are \UTILITY and \PUBLIC. If you try to run a program which is not in your current directory, DOS will look for that program in the subdirectories in your PATH command, and now will also look for them in these two subdirectories specified in the SEARCH command.

Creating Additional Network Drives

There are three basic reasons to create additional network drives:

* It is easier to type H: and return to get to \USERDIRS than to have to type the entire path\directory name.

* You might have a program running in a subdriectory which wants to believe it is running in the root directory of a drive; you create a network drive to accommodate the desires of this program.

* It is more efficient to put H:\ in your PATH statement as opposed to putting the path\directory name for \USERDIRS since your PATH statement is limited to 127 characters and H:\ is only three characters and path\directory is usually going to be more than three characters.

You can use the MAP command to create additional network drives, and to extend the SEARCH command.

To MAP a drive to the \USERDIRS subdirectory on SYS, do the following:

1. Change to drive F: (or whichever drive is mapped first) by typing F: and pressing Enter.

2. Type DIR/P to make sure you have subdirectory \USERDIRS on SYS:. If not, use another subdirectory name.

3. Type MAP ROOT H:=SYS:\USERDIRS and press Enter.

4. Type MAP and press Enter to see your new MAPped drive (see Figure 2.3).

```
Drive  A:    maps to a local disk.
Drive  B:    maps to a local disk.
Drive  C:    maps to a local disk.
Drive  D:    maps to a local disk.
Drive  E:    maps to a local disk.
Drive  F:  = NETWARE_SERVER_1\SYS:           \
Drive  H:  = NETWARE_SERVER_1\SYS:USERDIRS   \
         ─────
SEARCH1:   = C:\
SEARCH2:   = C:\DRDOS
SEARCH3:   = C:\NETWARE
SEARCH4:   = Z:. [NETWARE_SERVER_1\SYS:     \UTILITY]
SEARCH5:   = Z:. [NETWARE_SERVER_1\SYS:     \PUBLIC]


C:\>
```

Figure 2.3   Drive MAPping for H:.

5. To include your new network drive H: in your search area, type MAP INS S10:=SYS:\USERDIRS and press Enter, and you now have another drive that DOS will search for programs you attempt to run (see Figure 2.4).

The network drive you just created with the MAP command is what is called a *logical drive*.

Very Logical   A *logical drive* is nothing more than a subdirectory that has been given a drive name, and that now functions like any other drive.

You can use the MAP command to delete network drives as well as create them. To delete the drive H: you just created, do the following:

1. Type MAP and press Enter to make sure the drive you want to delete still exists.

13

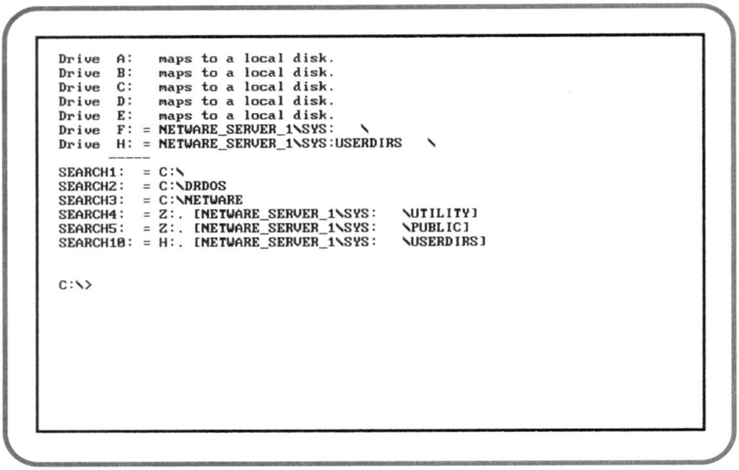

```
Drive  A:    maps to a local disk.
Drive  B:    maps to a local disk.
Drive  C:    maps to a local disk.
Drive  D:    maps to a local disk.
Drive  E:    maps to a local disk.
Drive  F: = NETWARE_SERVER_1\SYS:        \
Drive  H: = NETWARE_SERVER_1\SYS:USERDIRS    \

SEARCH1:   = C:\
SEARCH2:   = C:\DRDOS
SEARCH3:   = C:\NETWARE
SEARCH4:   = Z:. [NETWARE_SERVER_1\SYS:    \UTILITY]
SEARCH5:   = Z:. [NETWARE_SERVER_1\SYS:    \PUBLIC]
SEARCH10:  = H:. [NETWARE_SERVER_1\SYS:    \USERDIRS]

C:\>
```

Figure 2.4   Extending your search path to drive H:.

MAP DEL H:

2. Type MAP H: DEL and press Enter to delete your drive H:.

3. Type MAP DEL S10: and press Enter to delete your search drive.

4. Type MAP and press Enter again, and you will see that your drive H: and search drive are now gone (see Figure 2.5).

Even if you don't delete any drives you create, they will exist only until you log out of the system.

14

```
Drive  A:    maps to a local disk.
Drive  B:    maps to a local disk.
Drive  C:    maps to a local disk.
Drive  D:    maps to a local disk.
Drive  E:    maps to a local disk.
Drive  F: = NETWARE_SERVER_1\SYS:      \

SEARCH1:    = C:\
SEARCH2:    = C:\DRDOS
SEARCH3:    = C:\NETWARE
SEARCH4:    = Z:. [NETWARE_SERVER_1\SYS:    \UTILITY]
SEARCH5:    = Z:. [NETWARE_SERVER_1\SYS:    \PUBLIC]


C:\>
```

Figure 2.5   Drive H: deleted.

In this lesson, you have learned to display, create, and delete network drives using the MAP command. In the next lesson, you will learn how to automate the login process.

15

Lesson 3

Automating Your Login

In this lesson you will learn how to automate your login process.

Logging In Using AUTOEXEC.BAT

DOS runs two special files every time you start your computer—AUTOEXEC.BAT and CONFIG.SYS, stored in the root directory of your drive C:. DOS will execute every command in your AUTOEXEC.BAT file every time your computer starts (or *boots*). To log into your network automatically, it is a simple process to include the necessary commands in your AUTOEXEC.BAT file—and in this short lesson you will do just that.

Editing AUTOEXEC.BAT

To edit your AUTOEXEC.BAT file (or create one if you don't already have one), you will need a text editor.

No-Frills Text A *text editor* is simply a program that allows you to create plain text files—like a word processor, except it does not include in your file the "special codes" used for formatting or printing.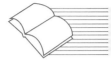

Some examples of text editors you can use are Brief, QEdit, TED, The Norton Editor, EDIT (if you are using DOS 5.0 or greater), and Editor (if you are using DR DOS). If you don't have any of these, or anything similar, you can use a word processor—provided it has a means of saving files in an ASCII format.

ASCII What? ASCII, which stands for the American Standard Code for Information Interchange, is just another way of saying plain text.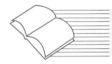

Saving Files If you use WordPerfect, save the files using Ctrl-F5 and not F10. If you use WordStar, use the N document option and not the D. If you use MS Word, save using the Save As Text Only option.

If none of these are available, you can always fall back on EDLIN, which is the line editor program which has been included with every version of DOS all the way back to version 1.0.

Whatever you decide to use for an editor, use it to open (or create, if necessary) your AUTOEXEC.BAT file. If you need to create AUTOEXEC.BAT, make sure you save it in the root directory of drive C: so DOS can find it.

17

The commands which you will be adding to your AUTOEXEC.BAT are:

`IPX`

`NET3` (or `NET4` for DOS 4, or `NET5` for DOS 5)

`F:LOGIN`

The first two are files which are stored on your computer. You need to know where these files are stored, so you can tell DOS where to find them. Do the following to locate these files:

1. Type `CD\`, then `DIR/P`, and press Enter to see if IPX.COM and NET3.COM (or NET4.COM or NET5.COM) are located in your root directory.

2. If IPX.COM and NET3.COM are not in your root directory, check to see if there is a subdirectory `\NETWARE` or `\NOVELL`.

3. If there is a \NETWARE (or \NOVELL) subdirectory, type `CD NETWARE` (or `CD NOVELL`) and press Enter.

4. Type `DIR/P` and press Enter to see if IPX.COM and NET3.COM are stored in the subdirectory.

All Right, Where Are They? If you can't find IPX.COM and NET3.COM, ask your network supervisor where they are located.

Once you've located IPX.COM and NET3.COM do the following:

1. Using your text editor, open AUTOEXEC.BAT.

2. Go to the bottom of the file and type the following command on a line by itself:

   CD\NETWARE

   (If \NETWARE is not the subdirectory where IPX.COM and NET3.COM are located, substitute the correct subdirectory name.)

3. On the next line add the command:

   IPX

4. On the next line add the command:

   NET3

5. On the next line add the command:

   F:LOGIN

6. Exit and save the file.

When you finish, your AUTOEXEC.BAT file should look something like the one in Figure 3.1.

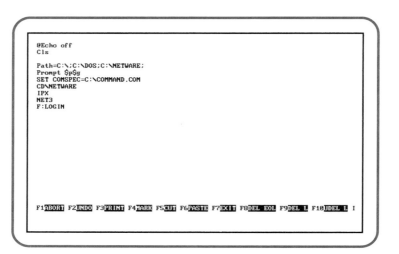

```
@Echo off
Cls

Path=C:\;C:\DOS;C:\NETWARE;
Prompt $p$g
SET COMSPEC=C:\COMMAND.COM
CD\NETWARE
IPX
NET3
F:LOGIN
```

```
F1 ABORT F2 UNDO F3 PRINT F4 MARK F5 CUT F6 PASTE F7 EXIT F8 DEL EOL F9 DEL L F10 UDEL L  I
```

Figure 3.1   AUTOEXEC.BAT with NetWare commands.

Editing CONFIG.SYS

There is also one command you need to check in your CONFIG.SYS file. Using the same text editor, do the following:

1. Open the file CONFIG.SYS.

2. Look for a command that begins LASTDRIVE= to see if it is set to E.

3. If it is not (or if the command is not in your CONFIG.SYS) on a line by itself, type:

   LASTDRIVE=E

4. Exit and save the file.

20

Your CONFIG.SYS file should now look similar to the one in Figure 3.2.

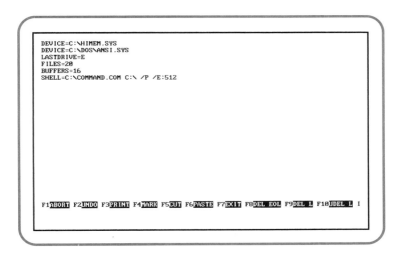

```
DEVICE=C:\HIMEM.SYS
DEVICE=C:\DOS\ANSI.SYS
LASTDRIVE=E
FILES=20
BUFFERS=16
SHELL=C:\COMMAND.COM C:\ /P /E:512
```

F1ABORT F2UNDO F3PRINT F4MARK F5CUT F6PASTE F7EXIT F8DEL EOL F9DEL L F10UDEL L I

Figure 3.2   Typical CONFIG.SYS file.

Don't worry about the other commands. If your CONFIG.SYS file includes them, fine—if not, they don't affect how NetWare operates on your computer. They are included for other programs or operations.

Testing Your File Changes

To test the changes you made in AUTOEXEC.BAT and CONFIG.SYS, do the following:

1. Reboot your computer by pressing Ctrl-Alt-Del.

2. At the Enter your login name: prompt, type your *user name* and press Enter.

21

3. At the Enter your password: prompt, type your *pass-word* and press Enter.

If everything worked, you should have logged into your network.

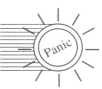

Can't Get There From Here   If you didn't log in, or if an error occurred, go back and check your AUTOEXEC.BAT and CONFIG.SYS files to make sure you entered the commands correctly.

In this lesson, you learned how to automate your login process by adding login commands to your AUTOEXEC.BAT and CONFIG.SYS files. In the next lesson, you will learn how to modify your NetWare environment and maintain network drives you create.

Lesson 4

Creating a User Login Script

In this lesson you will learn how to create a user login script.

Login Scripts

Login scripts are similar in operation to your AUTOEXEC.BAT file. When you start (or boot) your computer, your AUTOEXEC.BAT file runs and executes various commands to control your computer's environment. The same thing happens every time you login to NetWare. A *system login script* (created by your network supervisor) is run to control your network environment, usually creating the minimum number of network drives you will need. It might also launch a network menu program, and set certain access rights for each user.

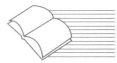

Environment? Your computer's environment pertains to certain configuration settings which effect how your computer will run certain programs or commands. To see part of your computer's environment, type SET and enter at any DOS prompt. Another part of your computer's environment is set by your

CONFIG.SYS file. You can see the contents of your CONFIG.SYS file by typing TYPE C:\CONFIG.SYS and pressing Enter.

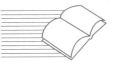

Access Rights *Access rights* are the amount of control the supervisor gives to each user over network resources. In effect, this is how you can use certain files, programs, or physical devices such as disk drives and printers.

In addition to the system login script, you can also create your own *user login script* to modify the environment set up for you by your network supervisor, provided your supervisor has given you access rights to modify your login script.

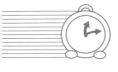

Ask First It's always a good idea to ask first, before you attempt to change anything about how your computer is set up. Just in case you discover something accidentally that was overlooked in your network security, you don't want to be responsible for "crashing the system."

Using SYSCON to Modify Your User Login Script

NetWare provides a utility called SYSCON, which allows users to modify their own user login scripts. SYSCON is stored in the \PUBLIC subdirectory during NetWare's installation. As you will see when you start SYSCON, it can be used to modify other user attributes and parameters besides the login script (see Figure 4.1).

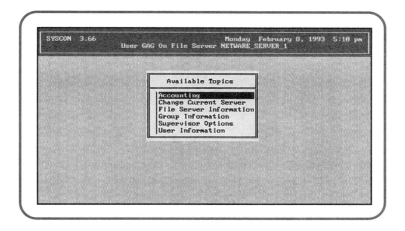

```
SYSCON  3.66                          Monday  February 8, 1993  5:18 pm
               User GAG On File Server NETWARE_SERVER_1




                         ┌─────────────────────────┐
                         │    Available Topics     │
                         ├─────────────────────────┤
                         │ Accounting              │
                         │ Change Current Server   │
                         │ File Server Information │
                         │ Group Information       │
                         │ Supervisor Options      │
                         │ User Information        │
                         └─────────────────────────┘
```

Figure 4.1   SYSCON's main menu.

Some of the options under SYSCON will not be available to you because they pertain to changing access rights, they can be used only by the network supervisor. For now we will concentrate only on the "User Information" option. Before we change anything in your user login script, let's first take a look at the options available to users. If you have not logged in, do so now.

1. Change to the \PUBLIC subdirectory by typing F: and pressing Enter.

2. Type CD\PUBLIC and press Enter.

3. Start SYSCON by typing SYSCON and pressing Enter.

4. Use the ↑ and ↓ keys to move the cursor down to User Information (the last selection on the SYSCON Main menu), and press Enter.

5. At the list of User Names, use the ↑ and ↓ keys to move the cursor to your user name.

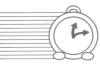

Quick Selection You can also press the first letter of your user name, and the cursor will move to the first user name which begins with that letter. For example, pressing G will take you to the first user name which begins with the letter G.

6. With the cursor on your user name, press Enter and the User Information menu appears (see Figure 4.2).

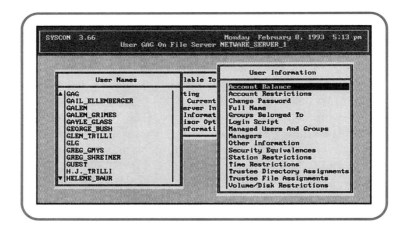

Figure 4.2 The User Information menu.

Before we make any changes to your user login script, take a few moments to look over the User Information menu. Your network supervisor used this same menu to set up your user account. Spend a minute looking over the information about your account; even if you don't understand all of it, you will gain more understanding of access rights.

Adding a Network Drive to Your User Login Script

1. Go back to the User Information menu in SYSCON by pressing ESC.

2. Use the ↑ and ↓ keys to move the cursor down to Login Script, and press Enter.

3. This will bring up your user login script. Don't worry if yours does not look just like the one in Figure 4.3.

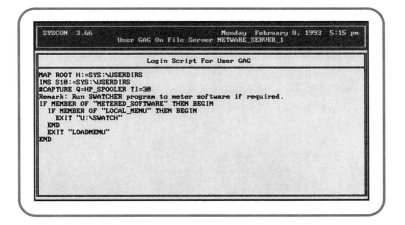

```
SYSCON  3.66                        Monday  February 8, 1993  5:15 pm
                 User GAG On File Server NETWARE_SERVER_1

                       Login Script For User GAG
MAP ROOT H:=SYS:\USERDIRS
INS S10:=SYS:\USERDIRS
#CAPTURE Q=HP_SPOOLER TI=38
Remark: Run SWATCHER program to meter software if required.
IF MEMBER OF "METERED_SOFTWARE" THEN BEGIN
  IF MEMBER OF "LOCAL_MENU" THEN BEGIN
    EXIT "U:\SWATCH"
  END
  EXIT "LOADMENU"
END
```

Figure 4.3   A user login script.

4. With the cursor on the top line, press Enter once so you can enter the drive-mapping command on the first line.

5. Type `MAP ROOT H:=SYS:\USERDIRS` and press Enter.

6. To add this newly-created drive to your search path, type `MAP INS S10:=SYS:\USERDIRS` and press Enter.

7. Press Esc to exit back to the User Information menu. Keep pressing Esc until you have exited SYSCON.

Now you need to test your modified login script.

1. Log out of NetWare by typing LOGOUT and pressing Enter.

2. Log in by typing LOGIN and pressing Enter.

3. At the prompts, enter your user name and password.

4. Type MAP and press Enter to see the network drive you've just added to your login script.

You can add virtually any NetWare command to your user script. To find out more about NetWare commands, there is another utility you can run.

1. Go to the \PUBLIC subdirectory by typing F: and pressing Enter.

2. Type CD\PUBLIC and press Enter.

3. Type HELP and press Enter. This starts the NetWare Help utility.

In a few seconds, the opening screen changes to the Help utility's Main menu (see Figure 4.4).

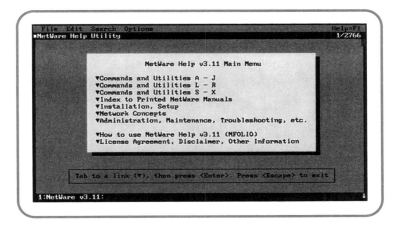

```
 File  Edit  Search  Options                              Help=F1
■NetWare Help Utility                                       1/2766



            NetWare Help v3.11 Main Menu

         ▼Commands and Utilities A - J
         ▼Commands and Utilities L - R
         ▼Commands and Utilities S - X
         ▼Index to Printed NetWare Manuals
         ▼Installation, Setup
         ▼Network Concepts
         ▼Administration, Maintenance, Troubleshooting, etc.

         ▼How to use NetWare Help v3.11 (MFOLIO)
         ▼License Agreement, Disclaimer, Other Information



     Tab to a link (▼), then press <Enter>. Press <Escape> to exit


 1:NetWare v3.11:                                              ↓
```

Figure 4.4   The Help utility's Main menu.

Most of the commands under "Commands and Utilities
A–J, L–R, and S–X" can be included in your user login
script. Before you add commands to your user login script,
try them first from the DOS prompt. Once you're comfort-
able with using them, you can add them one at a time.

In this lesson, you've learned how to add commands to
your user login script, and how to use the NetWare Help
utility to look up NetWare commands. In the next lesson,
you will learn how to use network printers.

Lesson 5
Using Network Printers, Part 1

In this lesson you will learn about network printers, and how to use them.

What Are Network Printers?

Up until now, you have probably used only what is called a *local* printer—one connected directly to your computer workstation. Direct connection means a physical cable runs from your computer to the printer, and nowhere else. With a local printer, you issue a command and your work is printed immediately—there is no waiting, nor do other users send their print jobs to your printer.

Network printers are attached to a network in a way that makes them available to multiple users. Dozens of printers of all types can be attached to a single network. On large or multiple networks, you could find over a hundred printers at your disposal. Network printers also employ a *print queue*, which allows multiple users to send an almost unlimited number of print jobs to a single printer.

What's My Queue? A *print queue* is a method for lining up multiple print jobs for printing. This order is usually FIFO, meaning **First In, First Out,** just like the checkout line at the grocery store. As each print job completes printing, the queue sends the next one to the printer.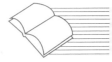

Using Network Printers

You have to know which printers are available to you on your network before you can start using them. Finding network printers means finding print queues. To find print queues:

1. Change to the \PUBLIC subdirectory by typing CD\PUBLIC and pressing Enter.

2. Type PCONSOLE and press Enter to start the printer console utility (see Figure 5.1).

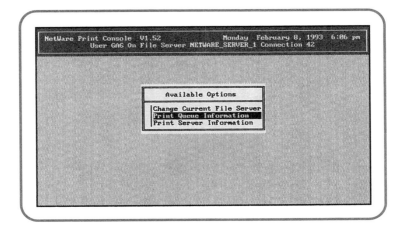

Figure 5.1   The PCONSOLE utility.

3. Use the ↑ and ↓ keys to cursor down to Print Queue Information, and press Enter.

A list of available print queues will be displayed, similar to the listing in Figure 5.2.

Figure 5.2 Print queues displayed in PCONSOLE.

Connecting to a Network Printer

Perhaps 90 percent of the network printing you'll do will be with the CAPTURE command, which connects your workstation to a network print queue. To connect to a network print queue:

1. Use PCONSOLE to locate the print queue you want to connect to.

2. Change to the \PUBLIC subdirectory by typing CD\PUBLIC and pressing Enter.

3. To connect to a network print queue, type CAPTURE Q=*queue name* (substitute the name of the print queue for ***queue name***).

In addition to the Q=*queue name* option, CAPTURE has other options you may need to use:

TI=*n*   where *n* is a number from 1–1000; this is the *Timeout* option. Use it to print from within an application program without exiting. (TI=30 is a recommended setting. Increase this number if only parts of your file are printing.)

L=*n*   where *n* is 1, 2, or 3. Use this option to designate a particular *local printer port* (LPT1:, LPT2:, or LPT3:). These are *logical connections*; it doesn't matter whether your local computer has the physical ports.

C=*n*   where *n* is the number of *copies* of the print job you want to print.

FF   is used to issue a *form-feed* at the end of the print job. This ensures that the next print job begins at the top of the page, and not where the current print job finishes. If you are printing from an application that issues its own form-feed, an additional blank page will follow your print job.

NB   is used to prevent the banner page from printing before the print job. A banner page is merely a page which identifies the print job and which user sent it.

NOT   asks that you be *NOTified* when your print job has left the queue and has been sent to the printer.

Printing to a Network Printer

Using a network printer is a little different from using a local printer; you are actually sending the print job to a print queue, instead of directly to the printer.

33

Don't be alarmed if you can see the printer from your workstation, and the print job does not begin printing immediately (as it would on a local printer). The print job is not sent to the printer until the print queue has received the entire job. Even so, when printing large jobs (especially if you are used to a local printer), you may be surprised at how quickly you can begin printing the next job.

Hang In There Some applications, if they are not designed to print over a network, may cause the print job to be suspended in the queue until you exit from the application.

Disconnecting from a Network Printer

Just as you issue a command to connect to a network printer, you also issue a command to disconnect. To disconnect, just type ENDCAP. (You can also use ENDCAP to force a print job to a printer if you have set the Timeout option too high.)

In this lesson, you learned how to locate and connect to network printers. In the next lesson, you will learn how to control print jobs in the print queue.

Lesson 6

More About Using Network Printers

In this lesson you will learn how to use PCONSOLE to control print jobs in print queues.

Queue Operators

Before you can control print (other than your own) jobs in a queue, you must be a designated *queue operator*. To find out if you are a queue operator:

1. Change to the \PUBLIC subdirectory by typing `CD\PUBLIC` and pressing Enter.

2. Start PCONSOLE by typing `PCONSOLE` and pressing Enter.

3. Use the ↑ and ↓ keys to move the cursor to Print Queue Information and press Enter.

4. At the list of print queues, use the ↑ and ↓ keys to move the cursor to the desired queue, and press Enter to display the Print Queue Information menu (see Figure 6.1).

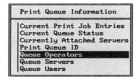

Figure 6.1   Print Queue Information menu.

5. Move the cursor to Queue Operators option and press Enter to display the list of print queue operators (see Figure 6.2).

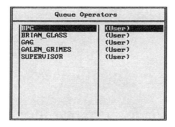

Figure 6.2   List of print queue operators.

If your user name is not on this list, contact your network supervisor and ask to be made a queue operator. Not being a queue operator means you can control only the jobs you send to the print queue. Queue operators can control print jobs sent by other users as well. Often network supervisors will designate someone in a department or workgroup as a queue operator to assist in managing the print queues. This is both a help to the department and the supervisor since it means that you do not have to track down the supervisor every time you want to move, delete, or hold a print job.

Nothing, short of incurring the wrath of the supervisor. Usually when this happens too often, users stop being queue operators. I think it might cause more panic than it would relief if we reveal this salient tid-bit.

Controlling Print Jobs

There are four categories of controlling print jobs:

- Changing parameters

- Changing the order in the queue

- Holding

- Deleting

Changing Print Job Parameters

Print job parameters are the parameters which affect how a print job is controlled by the print queue, such as, its order in the queue, how many copies will be printed, whether it is being held in the queue, whether a banner will print before the job, etc. In most cases, you will probably not need to look at them nor change them. But every so often, you will find that after sending a print job to the queue, you will change your mind about how the job is to be printed. This is when you will want to know how to change your print job parameters.

To change print job parameters:

1. Change to the \PUBLIC subdirectory by typing `CD\PUBLIC` and pressing Enter.

2. Start PCONSOLE by typing `PCONSOLE` and Enter.

3. Use the ↑ and ↓ keys to move the cursor to Print Queue Information, and press Enter.

4. From the list of print queues, select the desired queue and press Enter.

5. Select Current Print Job Entries and press Enter to display the current print jobs in the queue (see Figure 6.3).

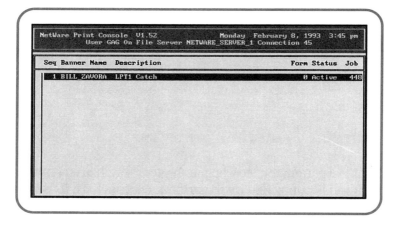

Figure 6.3   Listing of current print jobs.

6. Select the print job you want to change, and press Enter to display the Print Queue Entry Information screen (see Figure 6.4).

Changing the Order of Print Jobs

One of the more important tasks that queue operators perform is that of "bumping" a job up in the queue. To change the printing order of jobs in the queue:

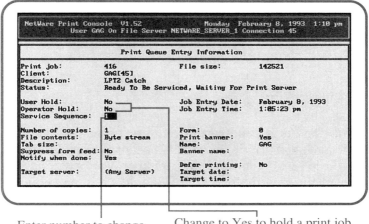

Enter number to change the order in the print queue.

Change to Yes to hold a print job.

Figure 6.4   Print Queue Entry Information screen.

1. Start PCONSOLE by typing PCONSOLE and Enter.

2. Use the ↑ and ↓ keys to move the cursor to Print Queue Information, and press Enter.

3. From the list of print queues, select the desired queue and press Enter.

4. Select Current Print Job Entries and press Enter to display the current print jobs in the queue.

5. Select the print job you want to change, and press Enter to display the Print Queue Entry Information screen.

6. Move the cursor to Service Sequence. To move this job to the top of the queue, type 1. (See Figure 6.4.)

The "top of the queue" means this job will print next. To move the job to other positions in the queue, type 2 for second, 3 for third, etc.

Holding Print Jobs

Sometimes it is necessary to hold a job in the queue to prevent it from printing—usually because at the last second you discover something (such as paper type or size) needs to be changed with the printer. To hold a job in the queue:

1. Start PCONSOLE by typing PCONSOLE and pressing Enter.

2. Use the ↑ and ↓ keys to move the cursor to Print Queue Information, and press Enter.

3. From the list of print queues, select the desired queue and press Enter.

4. Select Current Print Job Entries, and press Enter to display the current print jobs in the queue.

5. Select the print job you want to change, and press Enter to display the Print Queue Entry Information screen.

6. Move the cursor to either Operator Hold (if you are a Queue Operator) or User Hold, type Y for Yes, and press Enter (see Figure 6.4).

Deleting Print Jobs

Sometimes a print job is not needed, the wrong job was sent, or a user may request that a job be deleted. A queue operator can delete a job from the queue by following these steps:

1. Start PCONSOLE by typing `PCONSOLE` and Enter.

2. Use the ↑ and ↓ keys to move the cursor to Print Queue Information and press Enter.

3. From the list of print queues, select the desired queue and press Enter.

4. Select Current Print Job Entries, and press Enter to display the current print jobs in the queue.

5. Select the print job you want to delete, and press the Del key.

6. Select Yes in the Delete Queue Entry confirmation box. The job is deleted from the queue.

In this lesson, you have learned how to control print jobs in a print queue. In the next lesson, you will learn how to add network printer connections to your user login script.

Adding Network Printer Connections to Login Script

In this lesson, you will learn how to modify your user login script so it will connect you automatically to network printers when you log into the network.

The Difference Between CAPTURE and #CAPTURE

In Lesson 5, you learned how to use the CAPTURE command to connect to network printers, connecting to a network print queue by typing a command similar to this one:

CAPTURE Q=*queue name* L=1 TI=30

CAPTURE is both a command *and* an executable file. If you take a look in the \PUBLIC subdirectory, you will see an executable file named CAPTURE.EXE.

Executable? An *executable file* is simply a program that executes a series of commands. In DOS, most executable files have the file extension .COM or .EXE.

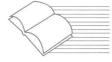

    Whenever you place the name of an executable file in a login script, you must precede it with the pound sign (#).

Not on the Map   The exception to this rule is use of the MAP command. If you look in the \PUBLIC subdirectory you will find it contains MAP.EXE, an executable file. But when MAP is used in a login script, it is used as MAP rather than #MAP.

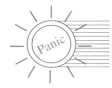

Using CAPTURE in Your User Login Script

CAPTURE follows the pound-sign rule. When you include it in your user login script, you use #CAPTURE instead of CAPTURE. To place the CAPTURE command in your user login script:

1. Change to the \PUBLIC subdirectory by typing F: and press Enter. Then type CD\PUBLIC and press Enter.

2. Start SYSCON by typing SYSCON and pressing Enter.

3. Use the ↑ and ↓ keys to move the cursor down to the last selection on the SYSCON Main menu (User Information), and press Enter.

4. At the list of User Names, use the ↑ and ↓ keys to move the cursor to your user name.

5. With the cursor on your user name, press Enter; the User Information menu appears.

6. Use the ↑ and ↓ keys to move the cursor down to Login Script, and press Enter. This procedure will bring up your user login script. Don't worry if yours does not look like the one in Figure 7.1.

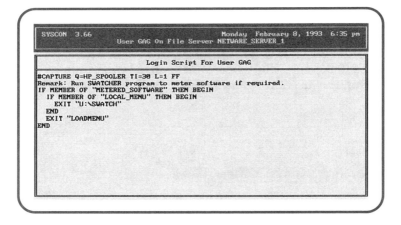

Figure 7.1   Sample user login script.

9. Press Enter to insert a blank line at the beginning of your user login script.

10. Type #CAPTURE Q=*queue name* L=1 TI=30 FF to connect *queue name* as your LPT1: port. If you want to connect an additional printer as LPT2: you would press Enter (to create a another blank line under this line) and type #CAPTURE Q=*queue name* L=2 TI=30 FF.

11. Press Esc, and at the confirmation Save Changes move the cursor to Yes and press Enter. Continue pressing Esc until you exit from SYSCON.

Since your user login script is read-only when you log in, testing the command you just entered requires that you log out, and then log in again. Type LOGOUT and press Enter to log out of NetWare. Now type LOGIN, press Enter, and at the prompts, enter your user name and password. As your login script is read, a confirmation similar to the one in Figure 7.2 shows you have connected to a network print queue.

```
Good morning, GAG.

You have Administration capabilities
Setting up access to Eq. Engr. Volumes . . . Stand By

Drive  A:  maps to a local disk.
Drive  B:  maps to a local disk.
Drive  C:  maps to a local disk.
Drive  D:  maps to a local disk.
Drive  E:  maps to a local disk.
Drive  F: = NETWARE_SERVER_1\SYS:   \
Drive  G: = NETWARE_SERVER_1\SYS:EQ-ENGR   \
Drive  S: = NETWARE_SERVER_1\SYS:SOFTWARE   \
Drive  U: = NETWARE_SERVER_1\SYS:LOGIN   \

SEARCH1:   = C:\
SEARCH2:   = C:\DRDOS
SEARCH3:   = C:\NETWARE
SEARCH4:   = Z:. [NETWARE_SERVER_1\SYS:   \SOFTWARE\SABER]
SEARCH5:   = Y:. [NETWARE_SERVER_1\SYS:   \UTILITY]
SEARCH6:   = X:. [NETWARE_SERVER_1\SYS:   \PUBLIC]
SEARCH7:   = W:. [NETWARE_SERVER_1\SYS:   \SYSTEM]
Device LPT1: re-routed to queue HP_SPOOLER on server NETWARE_SERVER_1.
```

Network printer connection

Figure 7.2   Connecting to network printer at login.

It Says So in the Script   If you don't get a confirmation similar to the one shown in Figure 7.2, or if you get an error message, go back into SYSCON and recheck your user login script to make sure you entered the command correctly. If everything looks OK, use PCONSOLE to recheck the name of the print queue you are connecting to. You can also check the status of CAPTURE by typing CAPTURE/SH at a DOS prompt.

The only thing left to do now is to send a print job to the printer. If you entered the command as it is shown above, anything you print to your first printer port (LPT1:) will be redirected to the network printer you connected to. Try first to print a simple text file, such as your CONFIG.SYS file. To print your CONFIG.SYS file, type `COPY C:\CONFIG.SYS LPT1:` and press Enter.

Go to the printer connected to the print queue you entered in your user login script, and see if there is a printed copy of your CONFIG.SYS file.

In this lesson, you learned how to modify your user login script to connect you to a network printer automatically. In the next lesson, you will learn how to send messages to other users on the network.

Lesson 8

Sending Messages Over the Network

In this lesson you will learn how to use the SEND utility to send messages to other users.

Network Messages

Besides the sharing of network resources (such as files, directories, and printers), NetWare offers the advantage of sending messages over the network to other users. The only real limitation is length of message—44 characters minus the length of your user name, which is included at the end of your message so the recipient(s) will know who sent it.

Don't confuse NetWare's messaging feature with electronic mail, or *E-mail*. E-mail (which is not a part of NetWare, but can be added when supplied by a third-party manufacturer) is a system of sending much longer messages to users; its capabilities include messages that can be stored, or accompanied by files at the sender's request.

Locating Users on the Network

Before you can send messages to other users, you must know who the other users are. NetWare supplies a utility called USERLIST which allows you to determine other users on the network. To use USERLIST:

1. Change to the \PUBLIC subdirectory by typing F: and pressing Enter, and then type CD\PUBLIC and press Enter.

2. Type USERLIST and press Enter to get the list of users currently logged into your default file server (see Figure 8.1).

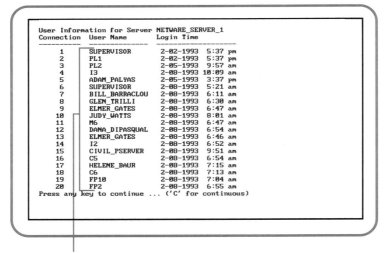

Users logged in to server

Figure 8.1 USERLIST display of users.

3. If there are multiple file servers on your network, first type SLIST and press Enter to get a list of all server

names (see Figure 8.2), then type USERLIST *fileserver/* and press Enter for each file server you find (be sure to replace *fileserver/* with the name of each server found by SLIST.

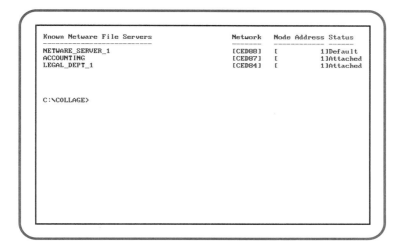

```
Known Netware File Servers                    Network   Node Address Status
-----------------------------                 -------   ------------ ------
NETWARE_SERVER_1                              [CED88]   [          1]Default
ACCOUNTING                                    [CED87]   [          1]Attached
LEGAL_DEPT_1                                  [CED84]   [          1]Attached


C:\COLLAGE>
```

Figure 8.2   List of file servers found by SLIST.

Locating Groups on the Network

You can also send messages to groups of users on the network.

What Are User Groups?   A *group* is a list of users who have been given the same access rights to a certain resource on the network. One example might be a group of users in ACCOUNTING_GROUP who have exclusive access to a network drive containing accounting data.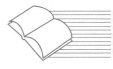

49

To find out which groups exist on a particular server:

1. Change to the \PUBLIC subdirectory by typing `F:` and pressing Enter, and then type `CD\PUBLIC` and press Enter.

2. Start SYSCON by typing `SYSCON` and press Enter.

3. Use the ↑ and ↓ keys to move the cursor down to Group Information, and press Enter (see Figure 8.3).

Figure 8.3   SYSCON showing list of groups.

4. To see who is a member of a certain group, move the cursor to one of the displayed group names, and press Enter to display the Group Information menu (see Figure 8.4).

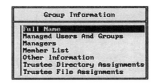

Figure 8.4   Group Information Menu.

5. Move the cursor down to Member List and press Enter (see Figure 8.5).

Figure 8.5 List of group members.

Other Groups If you need to identify groups on other file servers, go back to the SYSCON main menu and move the cursor to Change Current Server and press Enter.

Sending Messages Using SEND

Now that you've identified the users and the groups on your network, you can use the SEND command to send messages. Here's how to send messages:

Sending a Message to a Single User

1. Change to the \PUBLIC subdirectory by typing `F:` and pressing Enter, and then type `CD\PUBLIC` and press Enter.

2. To send the message `Staff mtg at 3pm.` to user JANIS_ WILLIAMS (for example), type `SEND "Staff mtg at 3pm." TO JANIS_WILLIAMS` and press Enter.

51

Sending a Message to a Group

1. Change to the \PUBLIC subdirectory by typing `F:` and pressing Enter, and then type `CD\PUBLIC` and press Enter.

2. To send the message `Staff mtg at 3pm.` to the ACCOUNTING_GROUP (for example), type `SEND "Staff mtg at 3pm." TO ACCOUNTING_GROUP` and press Enter.

Sending a Message to a User on Another Server

1. Change to the \PUBLIC subdirectory by typing `F:` and pressing Enter, and then type `CD\PUBLIC` and press Enter.

2. To send the message `Staff mtg at 3pm.` to BARB_BOYLE, a user on the ACCT_SRVR file server (for example), type `SEND "Staff mtg at 3pm." TO ACCT_SRVR/BARB_BOYLE` and press Enter.

In this lesson, you have learned to send messages to other users and groups using the SEND utility. In the next lesson, you will learn how to control message reception at your workstation.

Lesson 9

Controlling Message Reception

In this lesson you will learn how to control message reception at your local workstation.

Turning Message Reception Off with CASTOFF

When a message is sent to your workstation, no other instructions or programs can be run—or continued—until the message is cleared by pressing Ctrl-Enter. Sometimes, therefore, you will not want your workstation to receive messages sent from the server (e.g., warning messages) or from other users (with the SEND command).

Usually message reception is turned off because you are running a program you do not want interrupted (for example, a report that will run unattended for several hours or overnight). To turn off message reception:

1. Change to the \PUBLIC subdirectory by typing F: and pressing Enter, and then type CD\PUBLIC and press Enter.

2. Type CASTOFF and press Enter to turn off message reception from other workstations.

3. Type CASTOFF ALL and press Enter to turn off message reception from other workstations and messages sent from the file server.

Don't Add to Login Script   It is probably *not* a good idea to place a CASTOFF (or CASTOFF ALL) command in your user login script. There are times when it is important to receive messages, such as when the network supervisor plans to perform network maintenance (which requires the file server to shut down).

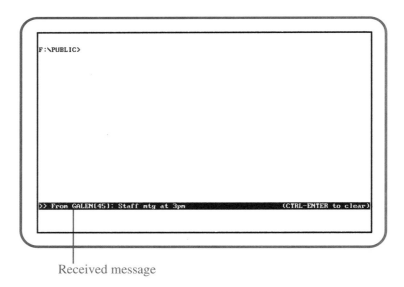

```
F:\PUBLIC>




>> From GALEN[45]: Staff mtg at 3pm                    (CTRL-ENTER to clear)
```

Received message

Figure 9.1   Message received at a workstation.

Restoring Message Reception Using CASTON

After you've used the CASTOFF command to turn off message reception at your workstation, you will want your workstation, at some point, to receive messages again. To turn message reception back on:

1. Change to the \PUBLIC subdirectory by typing `F:` and pressing Enter, and then type `CD\PUBLIC` and press Enter.

2. Type `CASTON` and press Enter to turn on message reception from other workstations and the file server.

After the CASTON command is entered you will receive confirmation that your workstation can once again receive messages.

In this lesson, you have learned to control message reception by using the CASTOFF and CASTON commands to turn message reception off and on. In the next lesson, you will learn about working with multiple file servers.

Using Multiple File Servers

In this lesson you will learn how to connect to and use multiple file servers.

Why Use Multiple File Servers?

Even though NetWare is licensed for up to 1,000 users per file server, you might not *want* that many (even on a high-performance 486 computer). Performance would be your first concern; a thousand users would bring a single PC file server to its knees. Network response time would suffer tremendously.

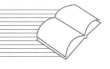

Hurry Up and Wait *Network response time* is simply how long you expect a task to be completed. An example is printing a one-page document. You would expect it to take no longer than 5–30 seconds. At 5 seconds, network response time is good; at 10 minutes, it's poor.

Dividing departmental tasks is another practical reason to use multiple file servers. One file server might be dedicated to accounting, another to the legal department or human resources.

You are likely to encounter multiple file servers as networks become larger and/or more specialized—so you will need to understand how to work with them. The latest release of Novell NetWare 386, version 3.11, requires that users have an account on each file server they intend to use. Make these arrangements with your supervisor.

Locating Multiple File Servers with SLIST

When you log into NetWare, you connect to the file server closest to your workstation—your *default* file server. To use other file servers on your network, you need to know their names. To find other file servers:

1. Change to the \PUBLIC subdirectory by typing `F:` and pressing Enter. Then type `CD\PUBLIC` and press Enter.

2. Type `SLIST` and press Enter to display a list of all file servers (see Figure 10.1).

Using Multiple File Servers with ATTACH

Once you've located the other file servers and set up your user accounts, you will want to connect to the other file servers. To do so, you would use the ATTACH command. For example, if you wanted to ATTACH to the AC-COUNTING file server found in Figure 10.1:

1. Change to the \PUBLIC subdirectory by typing `F:` and pressing Enter. Then type `CD\PUBLIC` and press Enter.

2. Type `ATTACH ACCOUNTING` and press Enter.

If you typed SLIST and pressed Enter again, it would not show you connected to the ACCOUNTING file server (see Figure 10.2).

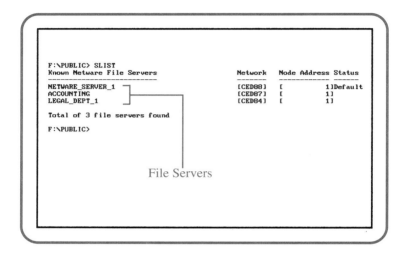

Figure 10.1 SLIST displaying all file servers.

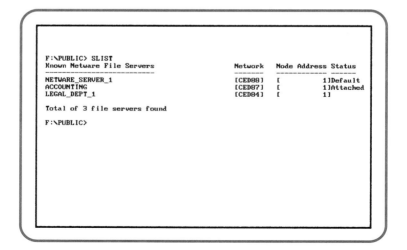

Figure 10.2 ATTACH to ACCOUNTING file server.

While the ATTACH command does connect you to additional file servers, it does not provide drive mapping (see Lesson 2, "NetWare Basics"). To see what drives are available on ACCOUNTING, follow these steps to MAP a drive to its SYS volume:

1. Change to the \PUBLIC subdirectory by typing `F:` and pressing Enter. And then type `CD\PUBLIC` and press Enter.

2. Type `MAP ROOT J:=ACCOUNTING/SYS:\` and press Enter.

3. Type `LISTDIR J:` and press Enter to list the directories available to you on ACCOUNTING.

Logging Into Multiple File Servers Automatically

If you make frequent use of file servers other than your default server, consider including ATTACH commands for them in your user login script (along with the appropriate drive-mapping commands). To include (for example) the commands for ATTACHing and MAPping to the ACCOUNTING server:

1. Change to the \PUBLIC subdirectory by typing `F:` and pressing Enter. And then type `CD\PUBLIC` and press Enter.

2. Start SYSCON by typing `SYSCON` and press Enter.

3. Use the ↑ and ↓ keys to move the cursor down to the last selection on the SYSCON Main menu (User Information), and press Enter.

4. At the list of User Names, use the ↑ and ↓ keys to move the cursor to your user name.

5. With the cursor on your user name, press Enter; the User Information menu appears.

6. Use the ↑ and ↓ keys to move the cursor down to Login Script and press Enter.

7. Press Enter to create a blank line. Type `ATTACH ACCOUNT-ING` and press Enter.

8. On the next line, type `MAP ROOT J:=ACCOUNTING/SYS:\`.

9. Press Esc to exit back to the User Information menu. Keep pressing Esc to exit out of SYSCON.

The next time you log in, you will be prompted twice for your password; providing it will connect you automatically to both your default server and the ACCOUNTING server—plus any other server(s) your supervisor has approved for your use, and you have included in your login script.

In this lesson, you have learned how to ATTACH to multiple file servers, and how to make these attachments a part of your user login script. In the next lesson, you will learn how to use the SESSION utility.

Lesson 11

Using the
SESSION
Utility

In this lesson you will learn how to use the SESSION utility to display and control the selection and usage of file servers.

Note: Any tasks you perform (or changes you make) using SESSION will remain in effect for your current network session; they last only until you log out. To make your changes permanent, consider adding them to your login script.

The SESSION utility is used to make temporary or "on-the-fly" changes to your current work session.

Using SESSION to Display or ATTACH to Another Server

You can use the SESSION utility to display other file servers, or to ATTACH to another file server:

1. Change to the \PUBLIC subdirectory by typing F: and Enter. And then type CD\PUBLIC and press Enter.

2. Start SESSION by typing SESSION and pressing Enter (see Figure 11.1).

61

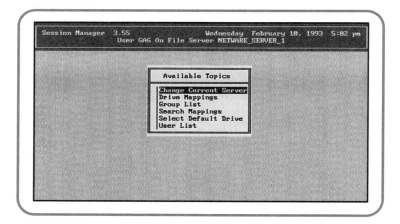

Figure 11.1   SESSION Main menu.

3. With the cursor on Change Current Server, press Enter.

4. The server you are currently logged into, along with your user name, is displayed (see Figure 11.2).

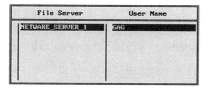

Figure 11.2   Currently-logged-in server.

5. Press the Ins key to display Other File Servers (see Figure 11.3).

6. Move the cursor to the file server you want to ATTACH to, and press Enter.

7. At the prompts, enter your user name and password.

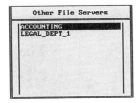

Figure 11.3   Other file servers available.

Using SESSION to Log Out of an Attached File Server

If you are attached to multiple servers, you can use SESSION to log out of any server except your default:

1. From the SESSION Main menu, move the cursor to Change Current Server, and press Enter to display the list of servers you are currently logged into.

2. Move the cursor to the server you want to log out of, and press the Del key. Answer Yes when asked for confirmation.

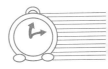

Adios, Amigos   To log out of multiple servers, mark each server by moving the cursor to it and pressing either F5 or F6. When you have marked all servers, press Del. Answer Yes when asked for confirmation.

In this lesson you have learned to use the SESSION utility to display, attach to, and log out of other file servers. In the next lesson, you will learn to use SESSION to control drive mapping.

Lesson 12

Using SESSION for Mapping Drives

In this lesson you will learn how to use the SESSION utility to control drive mapping.

Using SESSION for Network Drive Mapping

You can also use SESSION to control drive mapping. You can display mapping, map a new drive, delete or modify drive mapping.

Displaying Drive Mapping

To use SESSION to display the list of your currently mapped drives:

1. Change to the \PUBLIC subdirectory by typing F: and Enter. And then type CD\PUBLIC and Enter.

2. Start SESSION by typing SESSION and pressing Enter.

3. Move the cursor to Drive Mappings, and press Enter to display the list of your currently mapped drives (see Figure 12.1).

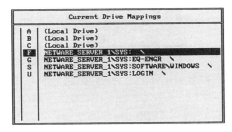

Figure 12.1   Display of mapped drives.

4. You can select any listed drive by moving the cursor to it and pressing Enter to display information about it (see Figure 12.2).

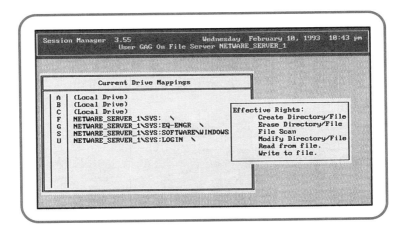

Figure 12.2   Drive information.

MAP a New Drive

To use SESSION to MAP a new drive:

1. From the SESSION Main menu, move the cursor to Drive Mappings, and press Enter to display the list of your currently mapped drives.

2. Press Ins and the next available drive letter appears (see Figure 12.3). You can use this letter for your next mapped drive, or type in a new drive letter.

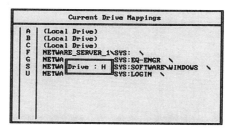

Figure 12.3   Next available drive letter.

3. Press Enter and the Select Directory entry box is displayed (see Figure 12.4).

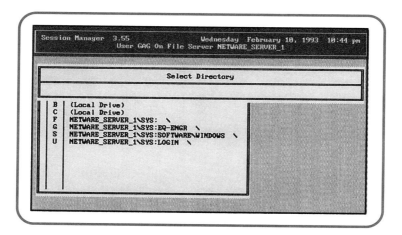

Figure 12.4   Select Directory entry box.

4. If you know the name of the directory you want to map, type it in and press Enter. If you do not, press Ins to display your default server.

5. Press Enter to display the volume(s) on your default server (see Figure 12.5).

Figure 12.5   Volume(s) on the default server.

6. Move the cursor to the correct volume; press Enter to display the directories on that volume (see Figure 12.6).

Figure 12.6   Directories on chosen volume.

7. Move the cursor to the directory you want to map, and press Enter. Repeat if you want to map to a subdirectory.

8. When you have entered the complete directory path into the Select Directory box, press Esc.

9. Press Enter and a confirmation box appears, asking if you want to map this drive as a root drive. Move the cursor to either Yes or No, and press Enter.

67

Delete a Mapped Drive

To use SESSION to delete a mapped drive:

1. From the SESSION Main menu, move the cursor to Drive Mappings, and press Enter to display the list of your currently mapped drives.

2. Move the cursor to the drive you want to delete, and press Del. Answer Yes or No in the confirmation box, and press Enter.

Take 'Em Out   To delete multiple drives, mark each drive by moving the cursor to it and pressing either F5 or F6. When you have marked all drives, press Del. Answer Yes when asked for confirmation.

Modify a Mapped Drive

To use SESSION to modify a mapped drive:

1. From the SESSION Main menu, move the cursor to Drive Mappings, and press Enter to display the list of your currently mapped drives.

2. Move the cursor to the drive you want to modify, and press F3.

3. Use the Backspace key to erase the portion of the drive mapping you want to change.

4. If you know the name of the server, volume, or directory you want to enter, type it in. If you do not know, repeat steps 4 to 9 under "Map a New Drive" in this lesson.

Using SESSION for Search Drive Mapping

You can also use SESSION to control search drive mapping.

Search Me Your *search drive* is created by using the MAP command. It's another place DOS will look for a program to execute if it has not found one in your current directory. A search drive is just an extension of your DOS PATH.

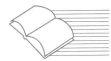

Display Search Drive Mapping

To use SESSION to display the list of your currently mapped search drives:

1. From the SESSION Main menu, move the cursor to Search Mappings, and press Enter to display the list of your currently mapped search drives (see Figure 12.7).

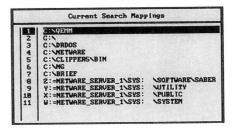

Current Search Mappings	
1	C:\QEMM
2	C:\
3	C:\DRDOS
4	C:\NETWARE
5	C:\CLIPPER5\BIN
6	C:\NG
7	C:\BRIEF
8	Z:=NETWARE_SERVER_1\SYS: \SOFTWARE\SABER
9	Y:=NETWARE_SERVER_1\SYS: \UTILITY
10	X:=NETWARE_SERVER_1\SYS: \PUBLIC
11	W:=NETWARE_SERVER_1\SYS: \SYSTEM

Figure 12.7   Display of mapped search drives.

2. You can select any listed drive by moving the cursor to it and pressing Enter to display information about it (see Figure 12.8).

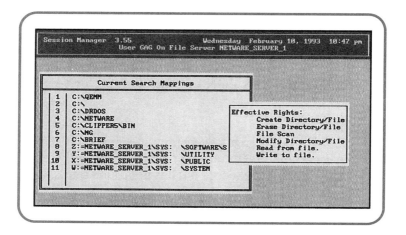

Figure 12.8 Drive information.

Add a New Search Drive

To use SESSION to MAP a new search drive:

1. From the SESSION Main menu, move the cursor to Search Mappings, and press Enter to display the list of your currently mapped search drives.

2. Repeat the steps under "Map a New Drive" in this lesson.

Modify a Search Drive Mapping

1. From the SESSION Main menu, move the cursor to Search Mappings and press Enter to display the list of your currently mapped search drives.

2. Repeat the steps under "Modify a Mapped Drive" in this lesson.

Delete a Search Drive Mapping

To use SESSION to delete a mapped search drive:

1. From the SESSION main menu, move the cursor to Drive Mappings and press Enter to display the list of your currently mapped drives.

2. Repeat the steps under "Delete a Mapped Drive" in this lesson.

Change Your Default Drive

The drive on which you are currently working is your *default drive*. When you execute a NetWare or DOS command (or executable program), your default drive is searched first. To change your default drive:

1. From the SESSION Main menu, move the cursor to Select Default Drive, and press Enter to display the list of your currently mapped drives.

2. Move the cursor to another drive and press Enter.

In this lesson, you have learned how to use the SESSION utility to control drive mappings. In the next lesson, you will continue with SESSION and learn how to use it for user and group tasks.

Using SESSION to Control User- and Group-Related Tasks

In this lesson you will learn how to use the SESSION utility to control user- and group-related tasks.

Just This Session *Remember:* any tasks you perform (and any changes you make) using SESSION will remain in effect during your current session, and last only until you log out. To make your changes permanent, consider including them in your login script.

Using SESSION to Control Group Tasks

SESSION can be used to control some group-related tasks, such as displaying the list of groups on your current file server and sending messages to group members.

Displaying Groups

To display the list of groups on the current file server:

1. Change to the \PUBLIC subdirectory by typing `F:`, pressing Enter, typing `CD\PUBLIC`, and pressing Enter.

2. Start SESSION by typing `SESSION` and pressing Enter.

3. With the cursor on Group List, press Enter to display the list of groups on the current server (see Figure 13.1).

Figure 13.1   Display of the current groups.

Sending a Message to a Group

You can use SESSION to send a short message (up to 55 characters including your user and connection number) to any group on the current file server:

1. From the SESSION Main menu, move the cursor to Group List; press Enter to display the list of groups on the current server.

2. Press F5 or F6, and then press Enter to select the group(s) you want to send a message to (see Figure 13.2).

Figure 13.2   Sending a message to a group.

3. Type your message (it can be up to 55 characters long, including your user name), and press Enter.

Using SESSION to Control User-Related Tasks

SESSION can be used to control some user-related tasks, such as displaying the list of users on your current file server and sending messages to individual users.

Displaying Users

To display the list of users on the current file server:

1. Change to the \PUBLIC subdirectory by typing F:, pressing Enter, typing CD\PUBLIC, and pressing Enter.

2. Start SESSION by typing SESSION and pressing Enter.

3. With the cursor on User List, press Enter to display a list of the current server's users (see Figure 13.3).

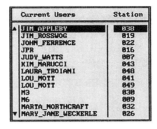

Figure 13.3   Display of the current server's users.

Display Information on Users

1. From the SESSION Main menu, move the cursor to User List, and press Enter to list the users on the current server.

2. Select the user you want to see, and press Enter.

3. Select Display User Information under Available Options, and press Enter (see Figure 13.4).

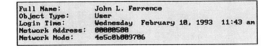

Figure 13.4   Information on a selected user.

Sending a Message to a User

You can use SESSION to send a short message (up to 55 characters, including your user name and connection number) to any user on the current file server:

1. From the SESSION Main menu, move the cursor to User List, and press Enter to list the users on the current server.

2. Select the user(s) you want to send a message to: press Enter, and then select Send Message under Available Options.

3. Type your message (up to 55 characters, including your user name) and press Enter.

In this lesson, you learned how to use SESSION to control user- and group-related tasks, and to send messages. In the next lesson, you will learn about user access rights.

Lesson 14
Understanding Access Rights

In this lesson you will learn about user access rights and how they affect and control your activities when logged in to NetWare.

The concept of "rights" can be confusing to new users. When your user account is first created, your network supervisor grants you certain *access rights* to the network resources you need to use. These can change from server to server, directory to directory, even file to file.

I Know My Rights Unless informed otherwise, you cannot change your access rights; only your network supervisor can. This lesson will show you how to view your rights; knowing them will help you diagnose the problem if a program doesn't work the way you expect.

There are eight categories of user access rights in NetWare, as shown in Table 14.1:

Table 14.1   NetWare's Access Rights

Type of Rights	Enable a User to ...
Supervisory	Grant all rights to the directory, its files, and its subdirectories; highest possible level.
Read	Read files in a directory and run programs.
Write	Open and modify a file.
Create	Create a file or subdirectory.
Erase	Delete a directory, its files, its subdirectories, and its subdirectory files.
Modify	Change file and directory attributes; rename a file or directory.
File Scan	See the files in a directory.
Access Control	Change the rights of a file or directory as they pertain to other users.

These rights can be given to any NetWare user. Often the network supervisor will give access rights to groups (instead of to individual users) according to need, and assign all users to one or more groups.

Using RIGHTS

NetWare supplies a RIGHTS utility, which allows you to examine your rights to both directories and files. To examine your rights for a given directory:

1. Change to the \PUBLIC subdirectory by typing `F:`, pressing Enter, typing `CD\PUBLIC`, and pressing Enter.

2. Type RIGHTS *path* (where ***path*** is the complete path to a directory or file), and press Enter. For example, RIGHTS F:\PUBLIC will produce a display similar to Figure 14.1.

```
F:\>rights f:\public
NETWARE_SERVER_1\SYS:PUBLIC
Your Effective Rights for this directory are [ R     F ]
    * May Read from File.                          (R)
      May Scan for Files.                          (F)
* Has no effect on directory.

    Entries in Directory May Inherit [ R    F ] rights.

F:\>
```

Figure 14.1 RIGHTS display of F:\PUBLIC.

To examine your right to a particular file:

1. Change to the \PUBLIC subdirectory by typing F:, pressing Enter, typing CD\PUBLIC, and pressing Enter.

2. Type RIGHTS *path\filename* (where **\path\filename** is the complete path to a file), and press Enter. For example, RIGHTS F:\PUBLIC\SYSCON will produce a display similar to Figure 14.2.

```
F:\>rights f:\public\syscon.exe
NETWARE_SERVER_1\SYS:PUBLIC\SYSCON.EXE
Your Effective Rights for this file are [ R    F ]
     May Read from File.                        (R)
     May Scan for File.                         (F)

F:\>
```

Figure 14.2   RIGHTS display of
F:\PUBLIC\SYSCON.EXE.

Using FLAG

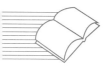

Characterize Your File   *Attributes* are charac-
teristics describing how files can be used; they are
needed to ensure that files are used on a network
only as intended. For example, the **R**ead **O**nly
attribute lets you see a file and read its contents, but
not change or delete it.

If you have **M**odify access rights, you can use FLAG to
view or change the attributes of files (listed in Table 14.2).

Table 14.2   NetWare's File Attributes

File Attribute	Definition
Archive Needed	Set to a file if it is modified after the last backup.
Copy Inhibit	Prevents a file from being copied (used only for Apple Macintosh files, not PC files).
Delete Inhibit	Prevents erasure of directories or files.
E**X**ecute Only	Prevents files from being copied (can be assigned only by the network supervisor, to .COM and .EXE files).
Hidden	Prevents the file from being shown by the DOS DIR command.
Index	Speeds file access for very large files (not user-assignable; NetWare assigns when needed).
Normal	Used to clear all attributes.
Purge	When assigned to a directory, prevents deleted files from being "unerased."
Read **O**nly	Prevents users from writing to, erasing, or renaming files.
Rename Inhibit	Prevents renaming files and directories.
Shareable	Allows a file to be used simultaneously by two or more users.
SYstem	Prevents the file from being shown by the DOS DIR command.
Transactional	Protects files from data corruption until all planned changes have been completed (usually applied to database files).

To view a directory's attributes:

1. Change to the \PUBLIC subdirectory by typing `F:`, pressing Enter, typing `CD\PUBLIC`, and pressing Enter.

2. Type `FLAG` *path* (where ***path*** is the complete path to a directory or file), and press Enter. For example, `FLAG F:\PUBLIC` will produce a display similar to Figure 14.3.

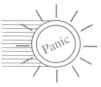

I Can't Change the Attributes   Unless your network supervisor has granted you **M**odify access rights, you will be able to use FLAG only to view file and directory attributes.

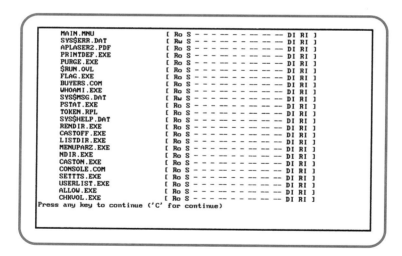

Figure 14.3   FLAG displaying attributes of F:\PUBLIC.

To use FLAG to view a file's attributes:

1. Change to the \PUBLIC subdirectory by typing `F:`, pressing Enter, typing `CD\PUBLIC`, and pressing Enter.

2. Type `FLAG` *path\filename* (where ***path\filename*** is the complete path to a file), and press Enter. For example, `FLAG F:\PUBLIC\SYSCON` will produce a display similar to Figure 14.4.

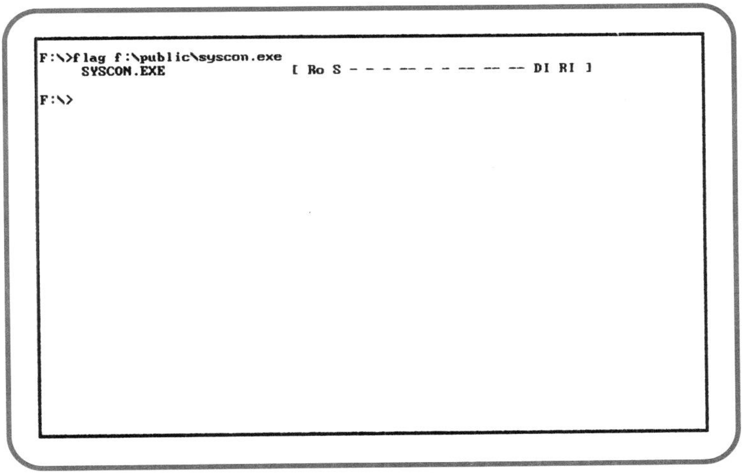

```
F:\>flag f:\public\syscon.exe
        SYSCON.EXE             [ Ro S - - - -- - - -- -- -- DI RI ]
F:\>
```

Figure 14.4   FLAG displaying attributes of F:\PUBLIC\SYSCON.EXE.

Using SYSCON to Check Restrictions

You can use SYSCON to check certain rights assigned to you by the network supervisor:

1. Change to the \PUBLIC subdirectory by typing `F:`, pressing Enter, typing `CD\PUBLIC`, and pressing Enter.

2. Start SYSCON by typing SYSCON and pressing Enter.

3. Use the ↑ and ↓ keys to move the cursor down to the last selection on the SYSCON Main menu (User Information), and press Enter.

4. At the list of User Names, use the ↑ and ↓ keys to move the cursor to your user name.

Take a Letter   You can also press the first letter of your user name, and the cursor will move to the first user name which begins with that letter. For example, pressing G will take you to the first user name which begins with the letter G.

5. With the cursor on your user name, press Enter; the User Information menu appears (see Figure 14.5).

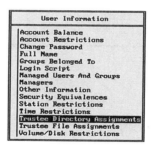

```
        User Information
  Account Balance
  Account Restrictions
  Change Password
  Full Name
  Groups Belonged To
  Login Script
  Managed Users And Groups
  Managers
  Other Information
  Security Equivalences
  Station Restrictions
  Time Restrictions
  Trustee Directory Assignments
  Trustee File Assignments
  Volume/Disk Restrictions
```

Figure 14.5   User Information menu.

The entries you want to check are:

• *Trustee Directory Assignments*   See in which directories your supervisor has granted you trustee rights on your file server.

- *Trustee File Assignments*   See if your supervisor has granted you trustee rights over any files on your file server.

In this lesson, you have learned about user access rights, and how they affect and control your activities when you log into NetWare. In the next lesson, you will learn about NetWare commands used specifically for directories.

Lesson 15

Working with Directories

In this lesson you will learn about NetWare commands used specifically for files and directories. Some of these commands are similar in operation to DOS commands, but are designed for use on NetWare file servers.

Using FLAGDIR

FLAGDIR is used to view or change the attributes of directories. Changes can only be made if you have Modify trustee rights. The attributes are described in Lesson 14, "Understanding Access Rights."

Unless your network supervisor grants you Modify trustee rights, you will only be able to use FLAGDIR to view directory attributes. To view a directory's attributes:

1. Change to the \PUBLIC subdirectory by typing `F:`, pressing Enter, typing `CD\PUBLIC`, and pressing Enter.

2. Type `FLAGDIR` *path* (where ***path*** is the complete path to a directory), and pressing Enter. For example, `FLAGDIR F:\PUBLIC` will produce a display similar to Figure 15.1.

Figure 15.1 shows that the directory \PUBLIC has "Normal" attributes, meaning that no other attributes have been set.

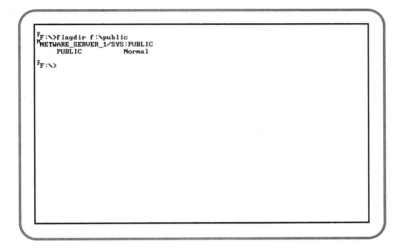

```
F:\>flagdir f:\public
NETWARE_SERVER_1/SYS:PUBLIC
     PUBLIC          Normal
F:\>
```

Figure 15.1   FLAGDIR displaying attributes of F:\PUBLIC.

Using LISTDIR

Unlike FLAGDIR (used to view attributes), LISTDIR is used to view your access rights in a directory. The format you will most likely use with LISTDIR is:

```
LISTDIR path ALL/
```

Typing this command will show you all your rights in the specified directory (*path*), along with its creation date and all subdirectories. To try LISTDIR:

1. Change to the \PUBLIC subdirectory by typing F:, pressing Enter, typing CD\PUBLIC, and pressing Enter.

2. Type LISTDIR *path* ALL/ (where ***path*** is the complete path to a directory), and press Enter. For example, LISTDIR F:\ /ALL will produce a display similar to Figure 15.2; the listing [SRWCEMFA] (or any combination of these letters) shows the attributes.

```
The sub-directory structure of NETWARE_SERVER_1/SYS:
Date       Time    Inherited     Effective   Directory
─────────────────────────────────────────────────────────
4-04-90   12:07p  [SRWCEMFA]  [ R    F ]  ->LOGIN
4-04-90   12:07p  [S       ]  [      F ]  ->SYSTEM
1-25-93   12:43p  [SRWCEMFA]  [      F ]  ->   E3020031.QDR
1-25-93   12:44p  [SRWCEMFA]  [      F ]  ->      PROCESSD
10-03-91   1:01p  [SRWCEMFA]  [      F ]  ->   SITELOCK
9-24-92    2:21p  [SRWCEMFA]  [      F ]  ->   A5020001
6-11-91    6:43p  [SRWCEMFA]  [      F ]  ->: ATPS
7-03-91    2:24p  [SRWCEMFA]  [      F ]  ->   07000006.QDR
7-03-91    2:49p  [SRWCEMFA]  [      F ]  ->      ELECTRI0
7-03-91    2:41p  [SRWCEMFA]  [      F ]  ->   98000002.QDR
7-03-91    2:49p  [SRWCEMFA]  [      F ]  ->      COMP
7-03-91    2:41p  [SRWCEMFA]  [      F ]  ->   06000007.QDR
7-03-91    2:49p  [SRWCEMFA]  [      F ]  ->      PIPINGCA
7-03-91    2:41p  [SRWCEMFA]  [      F ]  ->   00000006.QDR
7-03-91    2:49p  [SRWCEMFA]  [      F ]  ->      CIVILCAD
7-03-91    2:41p  [SRWCEMFA]  [      F ]  ->   99000005.QDR
7-03-91    2:49p  [SRWCEMFA]  [      F ]  ->      FAC.CAD
7-03-91    2:41p  [SRWCEMFA]  [      F ]  ->   98000005.QDR
7-03-91    2:49p  [SRWCEMFA]  [      F ]  ->      INSTR.CAD
1-28-92    5:09p  [SRWCEMFA]  [      F ]  ->   29020002.QDR
Press any key to continue ... ('C' for continuous)
```

Figure 15.2   LISTDIR displaying rights of F:\.

Using NDIR

NDIR (for Network **DIR**ectory) is similar to the familiar DOS DIR command, but NDIR is designed for NetWare and provides information DIR does not. NDIR is typed this way:

```
NDIR path /option
```

Multiple options are available for NDIR; Table 15.1 shows them. You can combine them as long as you remember to place a space after each option you use.

Table 15.1 NDIR Options

NDIR File Sort Options

(Type /REV in front of a file sort option to reverse its order.)

Option	Sorts files . . .
/SORT Owner	By file owner.
/SORT Size	Smallest to largest.
/SORT UPdate	By last modification date (earliest to latest).
/SORT CReate	By creation/copy date (earliest to latest).
/SORT ACcess	By last date accessed (earliest to latest).
/SORT ARchive	By last archive date (earliest to latest).
/UNsorted	(Will not sort files.)

NDIR File Format Options

Option	Sorts . . .
DATES	Files by last modified, last archived, last accessed, and last created dates.
/RIGHTS	Files by rights and attributes.
/MACintosh	Apple Macintosh files and directories; long file names (up to 31 characters).
/LONGnames	Macintosh, OS/2, and NFS (Unix) files by long file names.
/HELP	(Displays options.)

continues

89

Table 15.1 Continued.

NDIR Attribute Options
(Type /NOT before an attribute option to reverse it.)

Option	Function
/Read Only	Lists Read-only files.
/Shareable	Lists Shareable files.
/Archive Needed	Lists files which have the Archive attribute.
/EXecute Only	Lists files which are execute-only.
/Hidden	Lists Hidden files.
/System	Lists files which have the System attribute.
/Transactional	Lists Transactional files.
/Indexed	Lists NetWare-indexed files.
/Purge	Lists all files to be purged.
/Read Audit	Displays the Read Audit attribute (view only; not supported in NetWare version 3.11).
/Write Audit	Displays the Write Audit attribute (view only; not supported in NetWare version 3.11).
/Copy Inhibit	Sets "copy" rights of Macintosh files.
/Delete Inhibit	Prevents users from deleting files and subdirectories.
/Rename Inhibit	Prevents users from renaming files and subdirectories.

NDIR Restriction Options
(Type in the /NOT option to reverse the restriction.)

Option	Displays . . .
/OWner [/NOT] **EQ**ual to *name*	Files created by the user whose name replaces *name*.
/SIze [/NOT] **GR**eater than *nnn*	Files larger than *nnn* KB.
/SIze [/NOT] **EQ**ual to *nnn*	Files equal in size to *nnn* KB.
/SIze [/NOT] **LE**ss than *nnn*	Files smaller than *nnn* KB.
/UPdate [/NOT] **BEF**ore *mm/dd/yy*	Files last updated before the date *mm/dd/yy*.
/UPdate [/NOT] **EQ**ual to *mm/dd/yy*	Files last updated on the date *mm/dd/yy*.
/UPdate [/NOT] **AFT**er *mm/dd/yy*	Files last updated after the date *mm/dd/yy*.
/CReate [/NOT] **BEF**ore *mm/dd/yy*	Files created before the date *mm/dd/yy*.
/CReate [/NOT] **EQ**ual to *mm/dd/yy*	Files created on the date *mm/dd/yy*.
/CReate [/NOT] **AFT**er *mm/dd/yy*	Files created after the date *mm/dd/yy*.
/ACcess [/NOT] **BEF**ore *mm/dd/yy*	Files last accessed before the date *mm/dd/yy*.
/ACcess [/NOT] **EQ**ual to *mm/dd/yy*	Files last accessed on the date *mm/dd/yy*.
/ACcess [/NOT] **AFT**er *mm/dd/yy*	Files last accessed after the date *mm/dd/yy*.

continues

Table 15.1   Continued.

Option	Displays . . .
/ARchive [/NOT] **BEF**ore *mm/dd/yy*	Files last archived before the date *mm/dd/yy*.
/ARchive [/NOT] **EQ**ual to *mm/dd/yy*	Files last archived on the date *mm/dd/yy*.
/ARchive [/NOT] **AFT**er *mm/dd/yy*	Files last archived after the date *mm/dd/yy*.
/Files **O**nly	Only files.
/Directories **O**nly	Only directories.
/SUBdirectory	Subdirectories and subsequent subdirectories.

Two Examples of How to Use NDIR

- To display all files in F:\PUBLIC that are larger than 100,000 KB and sorted by size, type this line and press Enter (see Figure 15.3):

```
NDIR F:\PUBLIC /SI GR 100000 /SORT SI
```

- To display all files in F:\PUBLIC that are read-only and were created after 1/1/92, type this line and press Enter (see Figure 15.4):

```
NDIR F:\PUBLIC /RO /CR AFT 1/1/92
```

```
NETWARE_SERVER_1/SYS:PUBLIC

Files:                 Size      Last Updated        Flags               Owner
-------------          ----      ------------        -----               -----
VOLINFO        EXE     101,943   1-23-91   5:06p [RoS-------------DR] NETWARE_S
MENUPARZ       EXE     103,529   3-14-91   3:44p [RoS-------------DR] SUPERVISO
PSERVER        EXE     108,264   1-10-92  12:59p [RoS-------------DR] SUPERVISO
LOGIN          EXE     108,437   2-08-91   4:19p [RoS-------------DR] NETWARE_S
FOLIO          NFO     110,592   6-08-90   9:37p [RoS-------------DR] NETWARE_S
ACONSOLE       EXE     113,655   6-19-91   1:14p [RoS-------------DR] SUPERVISO
PVMANUAL       NFO     118,784   2-13-91  11:13a [RoS-------------DR] SUPERVISO
RTMANUAL       NFO     120,032   8-14-90  12:00a [RoS-------------DR] SUPERVISO
NCOPY          EXE     126,503   7-18-91  11:39a [RoS-------------DR] SUPERVISO
FCONSOLE       HLP     131,647   2-07-91  10:11a [RoS-------------DR] NETWARE_S
DSPACE         EXE     136,775   1-29-91   3:50p [RoS-------------DR] NETWARE_S
SALVAGE        EXE     143,553   1-30-91  11:56a [RoS-------------DR] NETWARE_S
SESSION        EXE     146,603   2-13-91  11:40a [RoS-------------DR] NETWARE_S
MAKEUSER       EXE     149,875   3-01-91  12:56p [RoS-------------DR] NETWARE_S
PRINTCON       EXE     160,823   1-26-91   7:50a [RoS-------------DR] NETWARE_S
USERDEF        EXE     180,627   2-06-91  11:27a [RoS-------------DR] NETWARE_S
BUYERS         EXE     184,503   8-14-90   0:00  [RoS-------------DR] SUPERVISO
PRINTDEF       EXE     192,203   2-11-91   4:52p [RoS-------------DR] NETWARE_S
NFOLIO         EXE     194,139   8-14-90   0:00  [RoS-------------DR] SUPERVISO

Strike any key for next page or C for continuous display...
```

Figure 15.3 NDIR displaying files sorted by size.

```
NETWARE_SERVER_1/SYS:PUBLIC

Files:                 Size      Created/Copied      Flags               Owner
-------------          ----      -------------       -----               -----
NET$PRN        OLD       8,910   1-27-92   8:59a [RoS-------------DR] JIM_ROSSW
NET$PRN        DAT       8,800   1-27-92   9:22a [RoS-------------DR] JPR
GRANT          EXE      41,555   8-05-92   3:37p [RoS-------------DR] SUPERVISO
MENU           EXE      32,709   8-05-92   3:37p [RoS-------------DR] SUPERVISO
MAP            EXE      40,053   8-05-92   3:37p [RoS-------------DR] SUPERVISO
FLAGDIR        EXE      32,309   8-05-92   3:37p [RoS-------------DR] SUPERVISO
MENUPARZ       EXE     103,529   8-05-92   3:37p [RoS-------------DR] SUPERVISO
SYSCON         EXE     200,049   8-05-92   3:37p [RoS-------------DR] SUPERVISO
NCOPY          EXE     126,503   8-05-92   3:37p [RoS-------------DR] SUPERVISO
RCONSOLE       HLP       9,147   8-05-92   3:37p [Ro--------------DR] SUPERVISO
RCONSOLE       EXE      83,391   8-05-92   3:37p [RoS-------------DR] SUPERVISO
ACONSOLE       EXE     113,655   8-05-92   3:37p [RoS-------------DR] SUPERVISO
PCONSOLE       EXE     233,873   8-05-92   3:37p [RoS-------------DR] SUPERVISO
RPRINTER       EXE      59,428   9-08-92   9:30a [RoS-------------DR] SUPERVISO
PSERVER        EXE     108,264   9-08-92   9:30a [RoS-------------DR] SUPERVISO
NOSTRTPG       PS          231   9-08-92   9:37a [RoS-------------DR] SUPERVISO
HIDE           PS          870   9-08-92   9:37a [RoS-------------DR] SUPERVISO
STRTPGON       PS          232   9-08-92   9:37a [RoS-------------DR] SUPERVISO
EHANDLER       PS        3,418   9-08-92   9:37a [RoS-------------DR] SUPERVISO

Strike any key for next page or C for continuous display...
```

Figure 15.4 NDIR displaying read-only files created after 1/92.

Using NCOPY

NetWare supplies its own version of the DOS COPY command, NCOPY (for Network **COPY**). NCOPY is used much the same as DOS COPY, except that NCOPY is guaranteed to preserve NetWare file attributes. The *command syntax* you type for NCOPY (slightly different from that of the DOS COPY command) is: *[***]*

```
NCOPY [path1][filename] [TO] [path2][filename][option]n
```

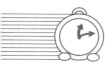

Really Wild Like the DOS COPY command, NCOPY also supports the DOS wildcard characters * and ? in place of *filename*. For example:
```
NCOPY F:\PUBLIC\*.EXE TO G:\USERDIR\GAG
```

To choose options to use with NCOPY, consult Table 15.2.

Table 15.2 NCOPY Options

Option	Definition
/Subdirectories	Use the /S option to copy subdirectories.
/Empty subdirectories	Use the /E option to copy empty subdirectory structures. It is only valid if you include the /S option.
/Force sparse files	Use the /F option to copy "sparse" files (usually database files that have areas where no data is written).

Option	Definition
/Copy	Use the /C option to copy files without preserving NetWare file attributes.
/Inform	Use the /I option to warn when you are copying files to an area which will not preserve NetWare attributes (e.g., a local drive, a drive on a non-NetWare file server).
/Verify	Use the /V option to verify that the copied file is identical to the original.
/A	Use the /A option to only copy files which have the Archive attribute.
/M	Use the /M option to copy files which have the Archive attribute (and to turn this attribute off for them).

An Example of How to Use NCOPY

- To copy all files in F:\PUBLIC which have the file extension .EXE to your local C: drive (and to be informed of any loss of NetWare attributes), type this line and press Enter (see Figure 15.5):

```
NCOPY F:\PUBLIC\*.EXE TO C:\ /I
```

95

```
F:\>ncopy f:\public\*.exe to c:\ /i
From NETWARE_SERVER_1/SYS:\PUBLIC
To    C:
      PRINTDEF.EXE   to PRINTDEF.EXE : DOS copy.
      PURGE.EXE      to PURGE.EXE    : DOS copy.
      FLAG.EXE       to FLAG.EXE     : DOS copy.
      WHOAMI.EXE     to WHOAMI.EXE   : DOS copy.
      PSTAT.EXE      to PSTAT.EXE    : DOS copy.
      RENDIR.EXE     to RENDIR.EXE   : DOS copy.
      CASTOFF.EXE    to CASTOFF.EXE  : DOS copy.
      LISTDIR.EXE    to LISTDIR.EXE  : DOS copy.
      MEMUPARZ.EXE   to MEMUPARZ.EXE : DOS copy.
      NDIR.EXE       to NDIR.EXE     : DOS copy.
      CASTON.EXE     to CASTON.EXE   : DOS copy.
      SETTTS.EXE     to SETTTS.EXE   : DOS copy.
      USERLIST.EXE   to USERLIST.EXE : DOS copy.
      ALLOW.EXE      to ALLOW.EXE    : DOS copy.
      CHKVOL.EXE     to CHKVOL.EXE   : DOS copy.
      PCONSOLE.EXE   to PCONSOLE.EXE : DOS copy.
      SYSTIME.EXE    to SYSTIME.EXE  : DOS copy.
      FLAGDIR.EXE    to FLAGDIR.EXE  : DOS copy.
      SETPASS.EXE    to SETPASS.EXE
```

Figure 15.5   NCOPY copying .EXE files to a local drive.

In this lesson, you have learned to use NetWare utility programs designed specifically to work with NetWare files and directories. In the next lesson, you will learn to use a few miscellaneous NetWare user commands.

Lesson 16
Miscellaneous User Commands

In this lesson, you will learn how to use some of NetWare's miscellaneous user commands.

Using WHOAMI

WHOAMI (Who Am I) is a NetWare command you can use to find out more about your user account. The syntax you type for WHOAMI is:

```
WHOAMI [fileserver] [option]
```

Use [*fileserver*] if you have accounts on file servers other than your default server. The options for WHOAMI are shown in Table 16.1.

Table 16.1   WHOAMI Options

Option	Definition
/Security	Use the /S option to examine your security levels.
/Groups	Use the /G option to see which groups you are a member of.

continues

97

Table 16.1   Continued.

Option	Definition
/**R**ights	Use the /R option to examine your rights on each file server.
/**W**orkgroups	Use the /W option to view workgroup manager information, if you are a workgroup manager.
/**SY**stem	Use the /SY option to view general system information.
/**A**ll	Use the /A option to combine all the other options.
/**C**ontinuous	Use the /C option to prevent the display from showing just one screenful at a time.

To see the WHOAMI information on your user account:

1. Change to the \PUBLIC subdirectory by typing F:, pressing Enter, typing CD\PUBLIC, and pressing Enter.

2. Type WHOAMI /A and press Enter (see Figure 16.1).

Using SETPASS

SETPASS is used to create or change your password on one or more file servers. You can also use SETPASS to synchronize your password so it is the same on all file servers. Passwords can be up to 127 characters long, but cannot contain control characters.

```
F:\>whoami /a
You are user GAG attached to server NETWARE_SERVER_1, connection 52.
Server NETWARE_SERVER_1 is running NetWare v3.11 (250 user).
Login time: Monday  February  15, 1993  7:32 am
You are security equivalent to the following:
    EVERYONE (Group)
    REGISTERED_USERS (Group)
    METERED_SOFTWARE (Group)
    ELECTRICAL (Group)
    WINDOWS_CAPABLE (Group)
    NETWORK_ADMINISTRATION (Group)
    COMPUTER_SERVICES (Group)
    EQUIP_ENGR (Group)
    FERROUS_R_MILLS (Group)
    MACINTOSH (Group)
You are a member of the following groups:
    EVERYONE
    REGISTERED_USERS
    METERED_SOFTWARE
    ELECTRICAL
    WINDOWS_CAPABLE
    NETWORK_ADMINISTRATION
    COMPUTER_SERVICES
    EQUIP_ENGR
Press any key to continue ... ('C' for continuous)
```

Figure 16.1 WHOAMI, displaying all your user information.

Control What? *Control characters* are special, non-printable characters (ASCII 0 to ASCII 31; see your NetWare documentation for a list). Often these are used to control functions on printers and other hardware devices. An example is ASCII 3 (created with Ctrl-C).

To use SETPASS:

1. Change to the \PUBLIC subdirectory by typing F:, pressing Enter, typing CD\PUBLIC, and pressing Enter.

2. Type SETPASS and press Enter.

3. Type your old password at the Enter old password for [file server]/[user name]: prompt.

4. If you did not have a password and are creating one, press Enter. If you are changing your existing password, enter your old password.

5. At the `Enter your new password for [file server]/ [user name]:` prompt, type your new password and press Enter.

6. At the `Retype new password for [file server]/[user name]:` prompt, retype your new password. (This security procedure ensures that you typed your new password correctly.)

7. Finally, you will get a confirmation message (see Figure 16.2):

   `The password for [file server]/[user name] has been changed.`

8. To synchronize your password on multiple file servers, log in as you would normally, ATTACH to the other file servers, and then use SETPASS. After the confirmation message appears, you will be prompted:

   `Synchronize password on these file servers? (Y/ N)`

   If you want to synchronize your password, type `Y` for Yes and press Enter.

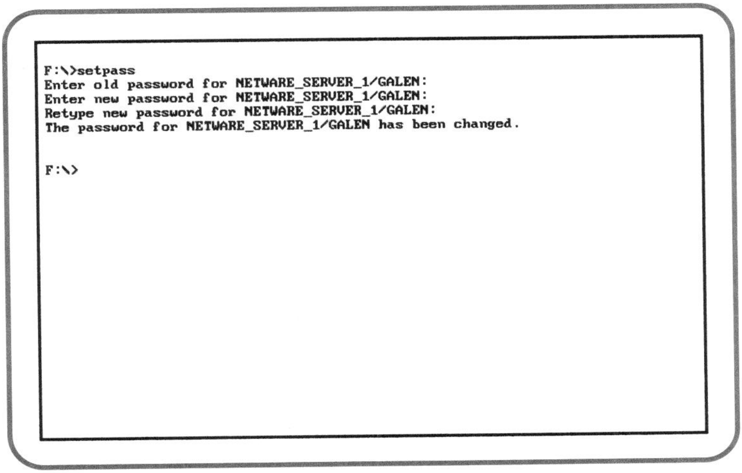

```
F:\>setpass
Enter old password for NETWARE_SERVER_1/GALEN:
Enter new password for NETWARE_SERVER_1/GALEN:
Retype new password for NETWARE_SERVER_1/GALEN:
The password for NETWARE_SERVER_1/GALEN has been changed.


F:\>
```

Figure 16.2   Using SETPASS to change your password.

Using SYSTIME

Use SYSTIME (for SYStem TIME) to view the system time and date settings on your default file server, or to synchronize the time and date on your workstation with those on the server. To use SYSTIME:

1. Change to the \PUBLIC subdirectory by typing `F:`, pressing Enter, typing `CD\PUBLIC`, and pressing Enter.

2. Type `SYSTIME` and press Enter (see Figure 16.3).

101

```
F:\>systime
Current System Time:   Monday  February  15, 1993  1:48 pm

F:\>date
Date: Mon  2-15-1993
Enter date (mm-dd-yy):

F:\>time
Time: 13:48:53.32
Enter time:

F:\>
```

Figure 16.3 Synhronizing date and time by using SYSTIME.

The time and date on your workstation are now synchronized with the time and date on the file server.

In this lesson, you have learned how to use some of NetWare's miscellaneous user commands. In the next lesson, you will learn how to use the NetWare SALVAGE utility.

Lesson 17
Using the SALVAGE Utility

In this lesson you will learn how to use the NetWare file SALVAGE utility.

Using SALVAGE

SALVAGE allows you to both recover deleted files on your file server, and to purge files that have been deleted. When you delete a file, the contents of the file are still present on the disk until that space is needed for another file, either a newly created file, or a file that has increased in size because more data was added to it. In order for SALVAGE to have the best chance at recovering a deleted file, it is best to use it to recover deleted files as soon as possible.

SALVAGE and Purging from Deleted Directories

If the directory is deleted (along with its file contents), the files are then stored automatically in the NetWare hidden directory called \DELETED.SAV. Every file server has a \DELETED.SAV, and SALVAGE can be used to recover these files. To salvage files from a deleted directory:

1. Change to the \PUBLIC subdirectory by typing `F:`, pressing Enter, typing `CD\PUBLIC`, and pressing Enter.

2. Type `SALVAGE` and press Enter. The SALVAGE Main menu is displayed.

3. Move the cursor to Salvage From Deleted Directories, and press Enter. If there are multiple volumes on your file server, you will be asked to select a volume.

4. In the Erased File Name Pattern to Match window, enter the name of the deleted file you want to recover. You can enter DOS wildcard characters "*" or "?" to recover multiple files. If you do not know the filename, press Enter to display all salvageable files (see Figure 17.1).

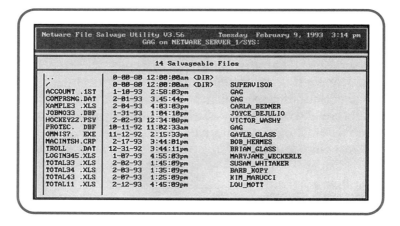

Figure 17.1   Display of all salvageable files.

5. Move the cursor to the file you want to recover; if you want to recover multiple files, use the F5 or F6 keys to mark the files, and select Yes from the confirmation box (see Figure 17.2).

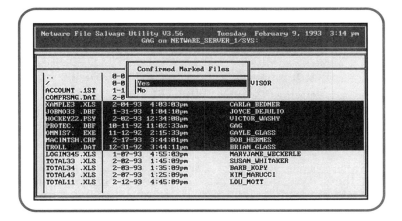

Figure 17.2 Recovering multiple files.

6. Once you have selected all files to recover, press Enter and select Yes from the Recover ALL Marked Files? confirmation box.

7. If instead you want to purge deleted files, follow steps 1–5 above, and instead of pressing Enter to recover files, press Del and answer Yes to the Purge ALL Marked Files? confirmation box (see Figure 17.3).

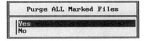

Figure 17.3 Purging files.

Be Very, Very Careful! Exercise caution when purging files! Once a file has been purged, it cannot be recovered—even with the SALVAGE command.

Select Current Directory

No Need to Start Up Again All NetWare utilities that modify files and directories have the Select Current Directory option, to make it easier to use the program in different directories. It lets you change to a new directory without having to exit the program.

Use the Select Current Directory option to change to a new default directory:

1. Start SALVAGE, move the cursor to Select Current Directory, and press Enter. If the directory path that appears is not the directory you need, press the Backspace key to erase the name, type the correct directory name, and press Enter. This becomes your new default directory.

2. If you are not sure of the directory name, press Ins to reselect file server, volume, and directory names.

3. Follow the steps under "View/Recover Deleted Files" in this lesson.

Set Salvage Options

SALVAGE also has a few options which can be set or changed to affect how it will display deleted files. To set this sort order:

1. Start SALVAGE, move the cursor to Set Salvage Options, and press Enter. The Salvage Options menu appears (see Figure 17.4).

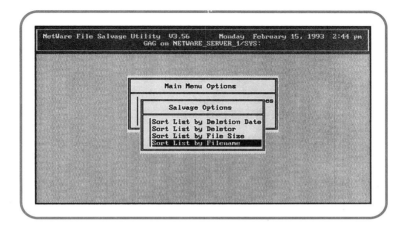

NetWare File Salvage Utility   V3.56   Monday February 15, 1993 2:44 pm
                           GAG on NETWARE_SERVER_1/SYS:

Main Menu Options

Salvage Options

Sort List by Deletion Date
Sort List by Deletor
Sort List by File Size
Sort List by Filename

Figure 17.4   Salvage Options menu.

2. Select the sorting method you want to use for salvageable files, and press Enter.

View/Recover Deleted Files

This option is used to recover files from a directory that still exists. If you want to attempt to recover files from a deleted directory, go back in this lesson to "Salvage From Deleted Directories."

1. Start SALVAGE, move the cursor to View/Recover Deleted Files, and press Enter.

2. In the Erased File Name Pattern to Match window, enter the name of the deleted file you want to recover. You can enter DOS wildcard characters, "*" or "?" to recover multiple files. If you do not know the filename, press Enter to display all salvageable files.

107

3. Move the cursor to the file you want to recover; if you want to recover multiple files, use the F5 or F6 keys to mark the files, and select Yes from the confirmation box.

4. Once you have selected all files to recover, press Enter and select Yes from the Recover ALL Marked Files? confirmation box.

5. If instead you want to purge deleted files, follow steps 2–4 above, and instead of pressing Enter to recover files, press Del and answer Yes to the Purge ALL Marked Files? confirmation box.

In this lesson, you have learned how to use the SALVAGE utility to recover and purge deleted files. In the next lesson, you will learn how to use the FILER utility.

Lesson 18

Using the FILER Utility, Part 1

In this lesson you will learn how to use the NetWare FILER utility.

FILER

The FILER utility is used to view and control volume, directory, file information, and access rights. It can also be used to change directory and file security rights. Unless you have supervisor security equivalence (which most users do not), some functions of FILER will not operate. Therefore, we will only cover the options you can perform with normal user rights.

Current Directory Information

Unless you have supervisor security equivalence, the "Current Directory Information" section will only allow you to view the currently selected directory. To take a look at the information it provides:

1. Change to the \PUBLIC subdirectory by typing `F:`, pressing Enter, typing `CD\PUBLIC`, and pressing Enter.

2. Type **FILER** and press Enter. The FILER Main menu appears (see Figure 18.1).

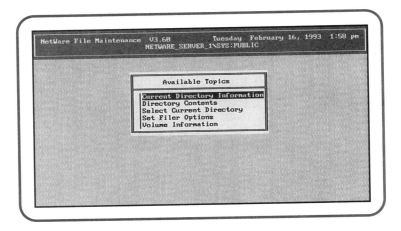

Figure 18.1   The FILER Main menu.

3. Move the cursor to Current Directory Information and press Enter to display the Directory Information for \PUBLIC (see Figure 18.2).

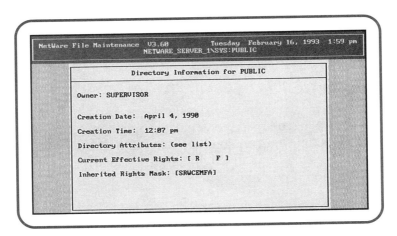

Figure 18.2   Directory Information for \PUBLIC.

Directory Contents

The Directory Contents section of FILER is used to view and manipulate directories and files (usually those in which you have more than read-only or file-scan rights). To use it:

1. Change to the \PUBLIC subdirectory by typing F:, pressing Enter, typing CD\PUBLIC, and pressing Enter.

2. Type FILER and press Enter. The FILER Main menu appears.

3. If you are not in your user or group directory, use the Select Current Directory option to change to it (see Lesson 19, "FILER, Part 2"), so you can work in a directory where you have full rights to files and directories.

It's My Default   The second line of the title bar at the top of the screen always displays your default directory.

4. Once you are in your user directory, move the cursor to Directory Contents and press Enter. The contents of your user directory are now displayed in the Directory Contents window (see Figure 18.3).

```
                    Directory Contents
..                              (parent)
\                               (root)
PKZ102                          (subdirectory)
TEST1                           (subdirectory)
ADDENDUM.DOC                    (file)
AUTHVERI.FRM                    (file)
COLLAGE.ZIP                     (file)
GALEM1_2.ZIP                    (file)
LICENSE.DOC                     (file)
MANUAL.DOC                      (file)
OMBUDSMN.ASP                    (file)
ORDER.DOC                       (file)
PK204E.EXE                      (file)
PKUNZIP.EXE                     (file)
PKUNZJR.COM                     (file)
```

Figure 18.3   The contents of your user directory.

111

5. Move the cursor to one of the files in your user directory and press Enter to display the `File Options` menu (see Figure 18.4).

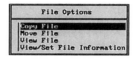

Figure 18.4 The File Options menu.

6. Using either Copy File or Move File will open a `Destination Directory` window. Type the directory path and press Enter to either copy or move the file. If you do not know the path, you can locate it the same way you did in the "Select Current Directory" section of this lesson, using steps 5–7 (see Figure 18.5).

Figure 18.5 The Destination Directory for Copy File and Move file.

7. Only use the View File option on a text file, since it opens the file for viewing (see Figure 18.6).

8. Finally, choosing the View/Set File Information option shows you information on the file (see Figure 18.7), allows you to change the file attributes and inherited rights, and shows you the list of file trustees if there are any.

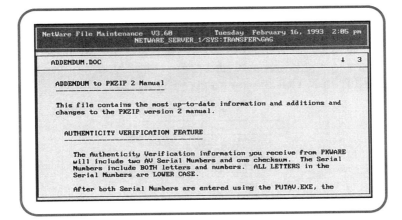

Figure 18.6   Viewing the text file.

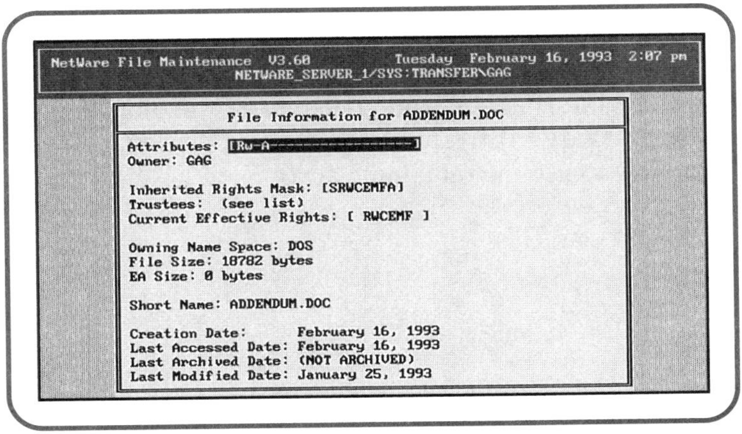

Figure 18.7   File Information.

Subdirectory Options

Just as in Step 5 of the previous procedure, if you move the cursor to a subdirectory and press Enter, you will get the Subdirectory Options menu (see Figure 18.8).

Figure 18.8   The Subdirectory Options menu.

Here the options for subdirectories operate along the same lines as the options for files. If you like, you can take a few minutes and peruse each of the subdirectory options.

In this lesson, you have learned how to use the "Current Directory Information" and "Directory Contents" options of the NetWare FILER utility. In the next lesson, you will learn how to use the remaining sections of FILER.

Lesson 19

Using the FILER Utility, Part 2

In Lesson 18, you learned how to use the first two sections of the FILER utility. In this lesson, you will learn how to use the remaining sections of the FILER utility.

Selecting the Current Directory

To understand how FILER works, you need to use it in a directory where you have—at least—read, write, create, and delete rights. On most networks, the supervisor usually provides each user (or group) a directory for storing files. Here is how you can use the "Select Current Directory" option to set your user or group directory as your default while in FILER:

1. Change to the \PUBLIC subdirectory by typing F:, pressing Enter, typing CD\PUBLIC, and pressing Enter.

2. Type FILER and press Enter to start the FILER utility.

3. Move the cursor to Select Current Directory and press Enter.

4. If you know the path to your user directory, type the full path name (*server*/volume/path) and press Enter. If you do not know the path, and you started from F:\PUBLIC, press Enter; the path to \PUBLIC should appear in the Current Directory Path window (see Figure 19.1).

```
                    Current Directory Path
NETWARE_SERVER_1/SYS:PUBLIC
```

Figure 19.1 The Current Directory Path, showing the path to \PUBLIC.

5. Press Ins and a window will appear showing Network Directories (see Figure 19.2).

6. Make sure the cursor is on the top line (the one showing the two dots). This indicates the parent directory.

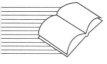

Not the PTA The *parent directory* is simply the first directory immediately above the one you are currently in. It is called the parent because all directories below it were created after it.

7. Press Enter to go to the parent directory. If your user directory (or its parent) was created off the root directory of F:, you should be able to move the cursor to it now. If not, repeat steps 6–7 until you find your user directory or its parent.

Take Me to My Directory If you still can't find it, ask your network supervisor for the path to your user directory.

8. Once you find your user directory (or its parent), move the cursor to it and press Enter. (If you are in the parent directory, you may have to repeat this step once or twice.) When your user directory appears in the Current Directory Path window, press Esc to close the Network Directories window.

9. Press Enter; your user directory should appear as the current directory. The path to your user directory should now be displayed on the second line of the title bar at the top of your screen (see Figure 19.2).

User Directory

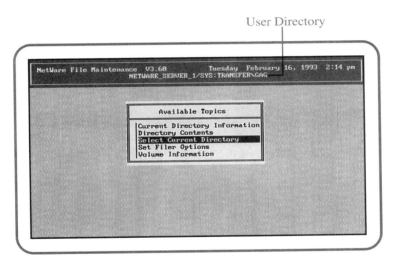

Figure 19.2 A title bar showing the user directory.

Setting FILER Options

The FILER options section controls the way FILER prompts you when you copy, delete, overwrite, or modify files, directories, or attributes. Most of the settings affect actions taken on groups of files and directories. To change FILER options:

1. Change to the \PUBLIC subdirectory by typing F:, pressing Enter, typing CD\PUBLIC, and pressing Enter.

2. Type FILER and press Enter to start the FILER utility.

3. At the FILER Main menu, move the cursor to Set Filer Options, and press Enter to change to the Options Set-up screen (see Figure 19.3). Select from among these options:

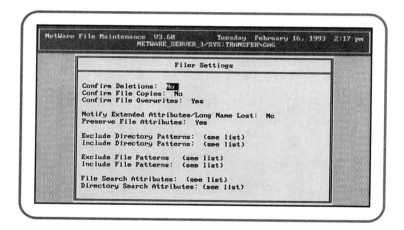

Figure 19.3 The FILER Options Setup screen.

• The setting Confirm Deletions: determines whether FILER will prompt you for every file or directory you delete, or just once for multiple files and directories. To change, type Y for Yes.

• The setting Confirm File Copies: determines whether FILER will prompt you for every file or directory

118

you copy, or just once for multiple files and directories. To change, type Y for Yes.

- The setting Confirm File Overwrites: determines whether FILER will prompt you for every file or directory you overwrite, or just once for multiple files and directories. To change, type N for No.

- The setting Notify Extended Attributes/Long Name Lost: is used to prompt you if you attempt to copy a file that will lose these attributes. To change, type Y for Yes.

- The setting Preserve File Attributes: is used to preserve the normal (read, write, etc.) file attributes. To change, type N for No.

- In the Exclude/Include Directory/File Pattern options, you can enter a pattern-match sequence (e.g., *.BAK, ART*.*, etc.) to include or exclude directories and files in the "Directory Contents" section.

- In the File/Directory Search Attributes section, you can determine whether file and directories with the attributes Hidden and System will be displayed in the Directory Contents section. (Normally, files and directories with Hidden and System attributes are not displayed.)

Volume Information

The Volume Information section merely displays information about the currently-selected volume on your default file server:

1. Change to the \PUBLIC subdirectory by typing F:, pressing Enter, typing CD\PUBLIC, and pressing Enter.

2. Type FILER and press Enter to start the FILER utility.

3. At the FILER Main menu, move the cursor to Volume Information and press Enter to change to the Volume Information screen (see Figure 19.4).

```
                    Volume Information
Server Name:                    NETWARE_SERVER_1
Volume Name:                    SYS
Volume Type:                    fixed
Total KBytes:                   262,148
Kilobytes Available:            219,816
Maximum Directory Entries:       53,824
Directory Entries Available:     25,849
```

Figure 19.4   The Volume Information screen.

In this lesson, you have learned how to use the rest of the NetWare FILER utility. In the next lesson, you will learn how to use NetWare's Help facilities.

Lesson 20

Using the NetWare Help Facilities

In this lesson you will learn how to use NetWare's Help facilities.

Command Line Help

There are two ways to obtain online help while in NetWare. The first is to use the *Command Line Help* facility:

1. Log into NetWare as you normally would, entering your user name and password when prompted.

2. At the DOS command line, type HELP [*commandname*] and press Enter. In place of [*commandname*], enter a NetWare command, (e.g., HELP CAPTURE, HELP WHOAMI, HELP MAP, etc.).

3. To get the Help screen shown in Figure 20.1, type HELP CAPTURE and press Enter.

Figure 20.1   The HELP CAPTURE screen.

NetWare Help Online Reference

The other part of NetWare's online Help facility is the *NetWare Help Online Reference*, which is a menu-driven utility. This is actually the same utility you call when you enter HELP [*commandname*], except now you are using its menu interactively. To start NetWare's interactive Help system:

1. Change to the \PUBLIC subdirectory by typing F:, pressing Enter, typing CD\PUBLIC, and pressing Enter.

2. Type HELP and press Enter; the NetWare Help system's Main menu appears (see Figure 20.2).

3. Press Tab to move the cursor to the line beginning Commands and Utilities A–J.

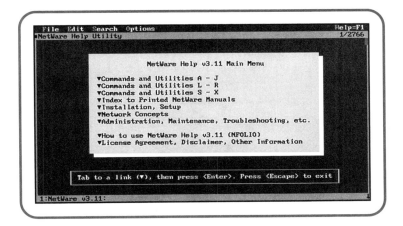

```
  File   Edit   Search   Options                          Help=F1
▪NetWare Help Utility                                        1/2766

                    NetWare Help v3.11 Main Menu

            ▼Commands and Utilities A - J
            ▼Commands and Utilities L - R
            ▼Commands and Utilities S - X
            ▼Index to Printed NetWare Manuals
            ▼Installation, Setup
            ▼Network Concepts
            ▼Administration, Maintenance, Troubleshooting, etc.

            ▼How to use NetWare Help v3.11 (NFOLIO)
            ▼License Agreement, Disclaimer, Other Information



         Tab to a link (▼), then press <Enter>. Press <Escape> to exit

 1:NetWare v3.11:
```

Figure 20.2   The Main menu for Interactive Help.

Tab Stop, Look, Read   At the beginning of each line, and throughout the Help system, you will notice a small, inverted triangle. Anywhere you see this symbol, you can Tab to this line and press Enter to obtain more information. At each lower level, if you see the symbol at the beginning of a line, it means that particular subject has been broken down into further sub-categories.

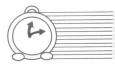

Navigating Help   Pressing Tab moves you in one direction through the menu screens. Pressing Shift-Tab moves in the reverse direction. On screens where the commands are in column form, use the arrow keys to move left or right.

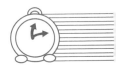

4. Once you obtain the information you want, press Esc to return to the previous screen. Pressing Esc at the Main menu takes you out of the program.

123

5. To look up the CAPTURE command (as we did before at the command line) at the Main menu, Tab to the line Commands and Utilities A–J, and press Enter to bring up the A–J commands (see Figure 20.3).

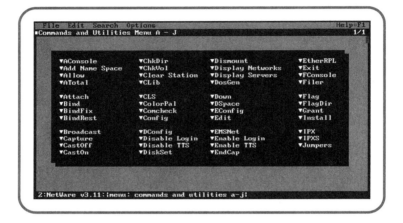

```
 File  Edit  Search  Options                                    Help=F1
■Commands and Utilities Menu A – J                                  1/1


        ▼AConsole          ▼ChkDir           ▼Dismount          ▼EtherRPL
        ▼Add Name Space    ▼ChkVol           ▼Display Networks   ▼Exit
        ▼Allow             ▼Clear Station    ▼Display Servers    ▼FConsole
        ▼ATotal            ▼CLib             ▼DosGen             ▼Filer

        ▼Attach            ▼CLS              ▼Down              ▼Flag
        ▼Bind              ▼ColorPal         ▼DSpace            ▼FlagDir
        ▼BindFix           ▼Comcheck         ▼EConfig           ▼Grant
        ▼BindRest          ▼Config           ▼Edit             ▼Install

        ▼Broadcast         ▼DConfig          ▼EMSNet            ▼IPX
        ▼Capture           ▼Disable Login    ▼Enable Login      ▼IPXS
        ▼CastOff           ▼Disable TTS      ▼Enable TTS        ▼Jumpers
        ▼CastOn            ▼DiskSet          ▼EndCap


    2:NetWare v3.11:¦menu: commands and utilities a-j¦
```

Figure 20.3   The A–J commands and utilities.

6. Move the cursor to the symbol in front of CAPTURE, and press Enter to display Help information on using CAPTURE (see Figure 20.4).

7. There is even help on using Help. Go back to the Main menu, move the cursor to the symbol at the beginning of the line How to use NetWare Help v3.11, and press Enter.

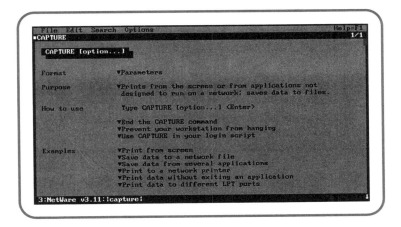

Figure 20.4 Help information on using CAPTURE.

Spend as much time in the Help section as you think you need, or to satisfy your curiosity.

In this lesson, you have learned how to use the NetWare help facility. In the next (and final) lesson, you will learn how to make changes in your workstation configuration files, to improve your PC's performance while in NetWare.

Lesson 21

Improving Workstation Performance

In this lesson you will learn how to improve the performance of your workstation when it is connected to a NetWare network. These suggestions are optional.

Upgrading to MS-DOS 5 or DR DOS 6

Many PC users continue to use MS-DOS version 3.3 as their workstation operating system. This is not unduly surprising, considering the overall stability and functionality of DOS 3.3, but if you are among those still using this version, you are severely limiting the potential of your networked PC.

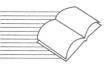

Thanks for the Memory *RAM*—Random Access Memory—is the type of built-in memory your computer uses to run programs. The amount your PC has is measured in kilobytes (K) or megabytes (M).

Upgrading to either MS-DOS 5.0 or DR DOS 6.0 (provided you are using a PC with an 80286 processor or higher) allows you to utilize a greater portion of your base 640K memory. Remember, in the DOS world, all programs still load and run in the first 640K of memory, regardless of how many megabytes of RAM are actually installed in your computer. This includes the portion of DOS that must be running in your computer in order to run DOS-based programs.

Under DOS 3.3, after booting your computer and loading DOS into memory, on the average you will have between 560–570K of RAM left out of your original 640K. With MS-DOS 5.0 or DR DOS 6.0, you can expect to have between 610–620K out of your original 640K of RAM, since both these operating systems allow you to load a large portion of DOS above the 640K mark.

Loading TSRs into High Memory

Once you've upgraded to either MS-DOS 5.0 or DR DOS 6.0, another adjustment you can make to improve the performance of your workstation is to load your TSRs into *high* (or *upper*) *memory*.

TSR?   TSR stands for Terminate and Stay Resident, and describes a type of DOS program that loads into memory, and instead of continuing to run, reverts to a sort of "dormant" stage, and returns control back to DOS. This allows you to run other programs; the TSR is still in memory, and ready to run when you press a certain key combination (which suspends the other program you are working in, and activates the TSR). Under DOS 3.3, TSRs are loaded into the base 640K of RAM.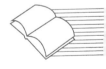

127

While there are limits to the number of TSRs that can be loaded into high memory, because the defined high memory area is not infinite in size. But remember, any TSR you can load into high memory will not be taking up part of your base 640K.

Loading NETx into Upper Memory

The improvements mentioned so far are all changes you can (and should) make to your workstation even before you look at connecting to a NetWare network. Back in Lesson 1, you learned that in order to connect to a NetWare file server there are three programs you need to run—IPX.COM, NET3.COM (or NET4.COM if you are using DOS 4.x, or NET5.COM if you are using DOS 5.0), and LOGIN.EXE. Of these three, IPX.COM and NETx.COM are both TSRs, but only NETx.COM can be loaded into upper memory. To load NETx.COM into high memory (above the 640K mark), you need to load in its place either EMSNETX.EXE or XMSNETX.EXE, depending on whether you have con-figured your upper memory area as either expanded memory or extended memory.

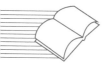

More, but Not the Same   *Expanded* and *extended* are terms used to describe the way memory above the 1-megabyte mark is set up and used. Both MS-DOS 5 and DR DOS 6 are capable of configuring high memory as either expanded or extended, de-pending on your needs and your programs. Run-ning Windows 3.x usually means configuring high memory as extended. By contrast, database or spreadsheet programs that use DOS text (such as dBase III/IV or Lotus 1-2-3) usually configure high memory as expanded.

Trimming Memory Usage in CONFIG.SYS

The final area you should look at when trying to improve the performance of your workstation is your CONFIG.SYS file. As mentioned in Lesson 3, the CONFIG.SYS file is one of two files DOS looks at every time you boot your computer. The CONFIG.SYS file (Figure 20.1 shows a typical example), is responsible for establishing certain configuration parameters; some of these affect and control workstation performance.

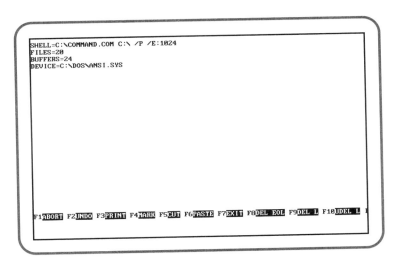

Figure 21.1   A sample CONFIG.SYS file.

Using the text editor you used in Lesson 3, open your CONFIG.SYS file and look for a line similar to this:

```
SHELL=C:\COMMAND.COM C:\ /P /E:1024
```

The last part of this line, /E:1024, can have an adverse effect on the amount of memory available to you if it is set too high. The only way to determine whether this is the case is to experiment with this setting. Try changing the 1024 parameter to a lower number, such as 512. Reboot your computer; as your AUTOEXEC.BAT file runs, watch to see if you get an error message saying Out of Environment Space. If you do, then the 512 parameter is too low. Adjust it up and reboot again. Keep adjusting the number, up or down, until you no longer get the error message. If you don't get the error message at 512, adjust it down slightly until the error message appears, then begin adjusting it up until you find the ideal setting for this parameter. To save time, adjust up or down by at least 10 or 20.

Look in your CONFIG.SYS file again for a line similar to:

    FILES=20

This parameter, too, can be set too high. (It is rarely set too low; since it affects the number of files a program can have open at once, many programs will not run if it is set too low.) Adjust it up or down, depending on your needs.

You should also check your CONFIG.SYS file for a line:

    BUFFERS=24

This parameter can also be set incorrectly. As a general rule of thumb, unless one of your application programs specifies a setting for this parameter, set it to run with your computer's processor chip:

    BUFFERS=8 for an 8088 (an IBM XT or compatible)

    BUFFERS=16 for an 80286 (an IBM AT or compatible)

130

BUFFERS=24 for an 80386 (needed to run Windows 3.x)

BUFFERS=32 for an 80486 (needed for a fast file server)

By now you'll notice that instead of accepting default settings for CONFIG.SYS parameters (and possibly wasting memory), you are attempting to "fine tune" these settings.

In this lesson, you have learned how to improve the performance of your workstation by fine-tuning memory usage, so as to make as much of your base 640K RAM available to your application programs.

Congratulations—you are now an experienced Novell NetWare user. But don't put the *10 Minute Guide to NetWare 3.11* on the shelf yet. Keep it near your workstation so you can use it as a fingertip reference whenever you have trouble remembering any of the commands and utilities covered in these lessons.

Appendix A

Networking
Primer

What Is a Network?

A *network*, also referred to as a *Local Area Network* (or LAN for short), is a system of computers connected by a combination of hardware and software. The connecting hardware consists of a *cabling* system and an *interface card*.

The cabling can be:

- *coaxial* (or "coax") cable, similar to the type used in cable TV.

- *twisted-pair*, the same type of 4-wire copper cable (two pairs of wires twisted together) used for telephones.

- *fiber-optic*, which uses glass or fiberglass instead of copper wire, to transmit light instead of electrical signals.

The *interface card* fits inside your computer (see Figure A.1) in one of the interface slots, and connects your computer to the cabling system; each computer on the network has one.

The software used on a network consists of two parts:

- the *network operating system* (in our case, NetWare version 3.11), which is installed on a computer designated as the *file server* (defined later in this appendix).

- the *client software*, which is installed on each PC *workstation* (any PC on the network that can use its shared resources).

What Is a Network Operating System?

The network operating system, often shortened to *NOS*, is a complex set of application software programs, used to control the sharing of network resources. These resources are:

- printers and other output devices

- hard disks

- directories on the hard disks

- files

- application software

The NOS is also responsible for maintaining *user accounts* and the *access rights* granted to each user account. Access rights (which most users relate mainly to file access), actually govern how each user may use any network resource. In addition, the NOS also has to arbitrate how each resource is used, whether it is a file (which can be shared by several users at once) or a device like a printer or modem (which can only accommodate one user at a time). As you can see, the NOS performs a multitude of networking tasks, and on large networks, often has to perform them for upwards of 200–300 network users at the same time.

What Is a File Server?

A Novell NetWare network is also referred to as a *client/server network* because it consists of one or more file "servers" (which run the network operating system software) and the "clients" (users on network-connected PCs) associated with each server.

Because it is used to control the sharing of network resources, and also as a large repository for file storage, the file server is usually the largest, most powerful computer on the network. Nowadays, most file servers are powerful 386 or 486 computers, with upwards of 16 megabytes of memory, and hard disks with capacities of gigabytes (1 gigabyte = 1000 megabytes).

NetWare has security features built into the system to prevent unauthorized users from tampering with the file server's configuration. Every so often a file server is locked away from its users as an added security measure, with access granted only to the network supervisor and the MIS or Computer Services staff.

Client Software

In comparison to the file server, the client PC needs minimal network-related software installed. On a Novell NetWare network, the client software consists of two programs:

- the *network protocol driver*, a program that ensures that the PC workstation and file server are both "speaking" the same network "language."

- the *NetWare shell*, which determines whether the local computer system performs a command (or function of an application program) or passes it on to the network.

Once these two programs load successfully and run on your PC workstation, all other network software—even the program used to log into the file server—are run from the file server. This arrangement ensures that any time a new version of NetWare is released, all workstations on the network can be updated with minimal effort, making it easier for the whole network to use the same (and most up-to-date) version.

Appendix B
DOS Primer

This section highlights some of the DOS procedures you are likely to encounter in a NetWare network whose computers use the DOS operating system.

Preparing Disks

The first step in preparing disks for storing programs and data is formatting the disks.

What Is Formatting? The *formatting* procedure writes important information on the disk, preparing it to store data. You can't place any information— programs or data of any kind— on a new disk before the disk is formatted. Formatting also erases any information on a previously used diskette. Do not format your hard disk drive, however, because formatting a hard disk erases all your programs along with the information on the hard disk.

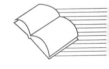

1. Turn the computer on.

2. If the system asks you for the date and time, type these in, and press Enter after each entry. (Not all systems ask for the date and time.) Enter the date in the form MM:DD:YY (such as `02:25:93`) and the time in the form HH:MM:SS (such as `5:45:00`).

3. When the DOS prompt is displayed (it will be shown as C>, D>, or A>, depending on the type of system you have and how it is set up), insert the first blank disk into drive A or B, and close the drive door.

4. Type the name of the drive where you inserted the blank disk, following the name with a colon (`A:` or `B:`, for example). Then press Enter.

5. Type `FORMAT A:` or `FORMAT B:` and press Enter. The system will tell you to insert the disk (which you've already done).

6. Press Enter. The system begins formatting the disk. When the format is complete, the system asks whether you want to format another.

7. If you want to format additional disks, type `Y` and repeat these steps.

Labeling Disks   While the disk is being formatted, you may want to use the time to write the labels for the disks. Be sure to write on the labels *before* you attach them to the diskettes.

Don't Point That Thing At Me   If you've already placed the labels on the diskettes, use a felt-tip pen to write on the labels—not a ballpoint. The hard point of a ballpoint pen can damage the surface of a diskette.

138

Working with Directories

DOS enables you to organize your files in *directories* and *subdirectories*. You can think of this organization as a "tree" structure—each directory can have subdirectories (like the branches splitting off from the trunk of a tree).

Making Directories

To create a directory, you use the MD (Make Directory) command. Follow these steps:

1. At the DOS prompt, type MD *directoryname.* (Substitute the name of the directory you are creating in place of *directoryname.*)

2. Press Enter.

This command causes DOS to create the directory under the name you specified, and places the new directory in the root directory.

Roots, Continued   The *root directory* is the main directory on your disk (the "trunk" of the "tree"). All other directories and subdirectories are divisions of the root directory. You may want to create directories for storing your data files.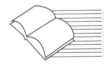

Moving to a Directory

You need to be able to move from one directory to another. To change directories, you use the CD (Change Directory) command:

139

1. At the DOS prompt, type CD*directoryname*. In this *command line*, the backslash (\\) tells DOS to begin at the root directory and move to the directory you specified under the root. You use the backslash to separate all directories and subdirectories in a command line. For example, if you wanted to move to a subdirectory of a directory, the command line would look like this:

   CD*directoryname**subdirectoryname*

2. Press Enter. DOS moves to the directory or subdirectory you specified.

Displaying a Directory's Contents

To see which files are stored in a directory, you use the DIR (Directory) command:

1. Change to the directory you want to display.

2. Type DIR.

3. Press Enter. DOS displays a list of all the files in the current directory.

Working with Files

DOS also includes commands you can use to work with the files you create. This section briefly introduces the procedures for copying, deleting, and renaming files.

Can't Get These to Work? Not everyone on a network is allowed to copy, delete, or rename files. If you try these procedures at your workstation and they don't work, see Lesson 14 ("Understanding Access Rights"), or consult your network supervisor.

Copying Files

When you want to copy files using DOS, you use the COPY command:

1. Move to the directory that stores the file(s) you want to copy.

2. Type COPY *filename1 filename2*. In this command line, *filename1* is the name of the existing file you want to copy, and *filename2* is the new name you want to give to the copy of the file.

   You can also copy a file to a different directory by typing

   COPY *filename1drivename\directoryname\filename*

   making the appropriate substitutions.

3. Press Enter.

Deleting Files

When you delete files using DOS, you use the ERASE (or DEL) command:

1. Move to the directory that stores the file(s) you want to erase.

141

2. Type one of these two command lines:

   ERASE *filename*

   or

   DEL *filename*

3. Press Enter.

4. When DOS asks you for confirmation, type Y. DOS then deletes the file.

Renaming Files

You use the RENAME (or REN) command to rename files in DOS:

1. Move to the directory that stores the file you want to rename.

2. Type one of these two command lines:

   RENAME *filename1 filename2*

   or

   REN *filename1 filename2*

   In these command lines, *filename1* is the name of the existing file, and *filename2* is the new name you want to assign to the file.

3. Press Enter. DOS renames the file, and keeps it in the current directory.

For more information about using DOS commands, consult *The First Book of MS-DOS* from Alpha Books.

Index

145

147

user accounts, information about,
      97-98
user login scripts, 24
   connecting to network printers
      automatically when logging
      in, 43-46
   logging in to multiple file
      servers automatically, 59-60
user names, 1-2
users
   determining access rights, 83-85
   displaying lists of, 74-75
   information about, 75
   sending messages to, 76
utilities, *see* programs

V-W

volumes, information about,
      119-120

WHOAMI command, 97-98
wildcard characters
   copying files, 94
   recovering files, 104
Word (Microsoft), editing text, 17
WordPerfect, editing text, 17
WordStar, editing text, 17
workstations, 134
Write access right, 78

X-Z

XMSNETX.EXE program, 128

149